JES

# Fostering Prayer

# Fostering Prayer
A 40 Day Guide for Foster Parents

Jessica Mathisen

JESSICA MATHISEN

Copyright © 2020 Jessica Mathisen

www.jessicanmathisen.com

All rights reserved. This book or any portion thereof may not be reproduced or used in any manner whatsoever without the express written permission of the publisher except for the use of brief quotations in a review.

Cover Design: Anna Crouse

Scripture unless otherwise noted, is taken from the Holy Bible English Standard Version, Copyright 2001 by Crossway, a publishing ministry of Good News Publishers.

ISBN: 9798550843376

# Table of Contents

Introduction ............................................................................................................... 7
Day 1: Abiding in the Spirit ............................................................................ 10
Day 2: Mental and Emotional Health ......................................................... 13
Day 3: Love ......................................................................................................... 18
Day 4: Joy ............................................................................................................ 21
Day 5: Peace ....................................................................................................... 24
Day 6: Patience .................................................................................................. 27
Day 7: Kindness ................................................................................................ 30
Day 8: Goodness ............................................................................................... 33
Day 9: Gentleness ............................................................................................. 37
Day 10: Faithfulness ......................................................................................... 40
Day 11: Self-Control ........................................................................................ 44
Day 12: Hope ..................................................................................................... 47
Day 13: Physical Health .................................................................................. 50
Day 14: Marriage .............................................................................................. 54
Day 15: Biological Children ........................................................................... 57
Day 16: Children in Care ................................................................................ 61
Day 17: Biological Parents .............................................................................. 65
Day 18: Judges ................................................................................................... 68
Day 19: Attorneys ............................................................................................. 71
Day 20: Counselors .......................................................................................... 75
Day 21: Social Workers ................................................................................... 78
Day 22: CASA Volunteers .............................................................................. 82
Day 23: Healthcare Providers ........................................................................ 85
Day 24: Fellow Foster Parents ....................................................................... 88
Day 25: Church Family ................................................................................... 91
Day 26: Outsiders Looking In ....................................................................... 95
Day 27: Spiritual Health ................................................................................. 98
Day 28: Surrender ............................................................................................ 101
Day 29: The Future .......................................................................................... 104
Day 30: Fear vs. Faith ...................................................................................... 107
Day 31: Thy Will ............................................................................................... 111
Day 32: Wisdom ............................................................................................... 115
Day 33: Forgiveness ......................................................................................... 118
Day 34: Humility .............................................................................................. 121
Day 35: Contentment ...................................................................................... 124
Day 36: Guilt and Shame ................................................................................ 127

Day 37: Boundaries .................................................................................. 131
Day 38: Grace of God ............................................................................ 134
Day 39: His Sovereignty ....................................................................... 137
Day 40: Facts vs. Truth ......................................................................... 141
Conclusion ............................................................................................ 144

# Introduction

*How did you and your husband begin to foster?* I get that question a lot. Many people wonder what made us say yes to this calling. Well, it was several things. On our very first date, we talked about how we both thought we would like to adopt one day. We didn't really know what we were saying or all that it would entail, but we knew we wanted to adopt children into our family. Fast forward nine months later, and we got married.

We had said that we would wait for a while before we had "our own kids." We were like a lot of people who are on our journey, thinking that it was important to establish "our own" family before taking other kids into our home. But boy did we have a lot to learn. When we had been married for about two years, we started trying to get pregnant, but nothing was happening. It was a dark and painful time for both of us, but God taught us so much. Through those sorrowful times we still thought about adoption. Then we went to a conference our church hosts every year for fostering and adoptive families. It was there that we learned about the foster care crisis in our state and in our nation. Our eyes were opened and the scales fell off. When we left the parking lot that day, we began to talk about what we sensed God was telling our family. Both of us said to each other, "I think we're supposed to foster."

We began the process a few months later and started filling out all the paperwork and taking the classes and doing the home study to open our home to children in need. We were so ready; scared, but willing.

Our first placement was a sibling group of three. We were definitely in over our heads. And it wasn't just because they were three of them and we were outnumbered! Their needs were great, their hearts were broken, and we were overwhelmed. We thought that we had done the work to be prepared and we thought that we knew what we were doing. In our naïveté and pride, we assumed that we could do a better job than their parents since these children were in care for a reason, right?

But oh how many slices of humble pie we ate when we realized that we were not their saviors. The only thing we could do was love them with the love of Christ and introduce them to Christ and know for sure that God loved them more than we did and that God had a better plan for them and that we just got to be a small part of it.

*Then the King will say to those on his right, "Come, you who are blessed by my Father, inherit the kingdom prepared for you from the foundation of the world. For I was hungry and you gave me food, I was thirsty and you gave me drink, I was a stranger and you welcomed me, I was naked and you clothed me, I was sick and you visited me, I was in prison and you came to me." Then the righteous will answer him, saying, "Lord, when did we see you hungry and feed you, or thirsty and give you drink? And when did we see you a stranger and welcome you, or naked and clothe you? And when did we see you sick or in prison and visit you?" And the King will answer them, 'Truly, I say to you, as you did it to one of the least of these my brothers, you did it to me.'"* - Matthew 25:34-40 ESV

Not only are we the hands and feet of Jesus, but when we

serve the least of these and the forgotten, we are serving Him. In the Christian life, we walk within a series of both-and paradoxes. What a joy, privilege and honor.

I am convinced that the power of prayer is real. We absolutely cannot love children who have come from hard places if we do not have the Holy Spirit's power working in us and enabling us to love them beyond our own capacities. When we do this, we must have an attitude of prayer. Prayer is what undergirds our decisions as we say yes or no to placements. It is how we have a strong marriage in the face of adversity. It is how our children's hearts are changed. There is no other way.

My hope as you read this book is that you understand the power that resides in your words. The power of death and life is on our tongues. How will we use it? I pray that you allow these 40 days to take you deeper into the heart of the Father as you seek to unite with Him in the work that He is already doing in the lives of the children that you serve and love every day.

# Day 1: Abiding in the Spirit

*As soon as Jesus was baptized, he went up out of the water. At that moment heaven was opened, and he saw the Spirit of God descending like a dove and alighting on him. And a voice from heaven said, "This is my Son, whom I love; with him I am well pleased." - Matthew 3:16-17, NIV*

Before Jesus began his three years of ministry, John the Baptist baptized him. During this beautiful baptism, we see the Holy Spirit descend on Jesus and anoint Him to do the work of the Father. During this baptism, Jesus receives a fresh indwelling of the Holy Spirit. It is only after this indwelling that He begins His earthly ministry. Everything He experienced up until that point was preparation for the next three years that led Him to the cross on our behalf. If Jesus Christ, the Son of God, needed a fresh indwelling of the Spirit for His earthly ministry, how much more do we? The calling to love children from hard places is not of this world. It is from Jesus Himself, who came to seek and save the lost. We cannot do this without Him. To abide in the Spirit means to dwell with Him.

*"But when the Helper comes, whom I will send to you from the Father, the Spirit of truth, who proceeds from the Father, he will bear witness about me. And you also will bear witness, because you have been with me from the beginning."*

John 15:26-27 ESV

**Prayer**

Today, let's pray for His Spirit to fill us anew.

Father, I thank You for the gift You have given me in Your Son. Thank You for calling me Yours. Today I am asking You to dwell in me anew. I am asking Your Holy Spirit to fall on me and make new wine. I need Your Holy Spirit's power, Father. I cannot do anything that is of eternal value without You working in and through me. Father, Your Holy Spirit is who called me to this journey. Thank You for giving me the courage to say yes. Please help me walk with You and dwell with You in order to be a vessel of Your love and grace. Empower me anew with authority to release Your peace and transforming love here on earth as it is in heaven.

**Scripture to Declare**

He who dwells in the shelter of the Most High will abide in the shadow of the Almighty. I will say to the Lord, "My refuge and my fortress, my God, in whom I trust." – Psalm 91:1-2, ESV

Already you are clean because of the word that I have spoken to you. Abide in me, and I in you. As the branch cannot bear fruit by itself, unless it abides in the vine, neither can you, unless you abide in me. I am the vine; you are the branches. Whoever abides in me and I in him, he it is that bears much fruit, for apart from me you can do nothing. - John 15:3-5 ESV

# Day 2: Mental and Emotional Health

*So Jesus said to the Jews who had believed him, "If you abide in my word, you are truly my disciples, and you will know the truth, and the truth will set you free." - John 8:31-32*

Over the past several years, mental and emotional health has been a topic of discussion within the mainstream media and also the church. With depression, anxiety, and suicide rates climbing, the awareness of the need for emotional and mental health is becoming much more prevalent within our society. God created us as whole beings—we are body, mind, spirit, and soul. What any one person sees when they look at us is only a glimpse of an exquisite masterpiece that God has created with intentionality.

When we choose to receive children from hard places into our hearts and homes, we are saying yes to a host of issues and strongholds that hold them captive and threaten to steal their very lives. We are also saying yes to their traumas and the behaviors that have manifested as a result. Each one of us has a story that has been written by our Heavenly Father. And if we are in Christ, we also have an enemy who is after us. He has stepped into parts of our story, and some of us may carry trauma and wounds of our own. If we are not aware of his schemes, we will not be able to walk in freedom and thus lead others to freedom.

Some of us are walking around with our pasts hanging over our heads, fearing that we will make the same mistakes or that we will be mistreated in the same way again. Others of us are so paralyzed by a fear of the future that we cannot see a way to get through the day that is before us. The children who come to us have been abused or neglected. They have not known stability. They have not known true peace. They have not known joy.

We are adults who are called to love and care for children from hard places. This means that we must first deal with our hard places. There are areas in each of our lives where we need healing. It could be wounds from our family of origin. It could be a life characterized by loss. It could be a chronic physical ailment. Each one of us has a place in our lives that needs the Savior's touch. The enemy of our souls wants us to believe that whatever we are facing, we are alone in it, and no one else has ever walked through what we have walked through. Our Savior brings us healing and hope when we choose to bring what is hidden in the darkness into the light. If we are struggling with intrusive thoughts, panic, worry, or debilitating fear, the only way to face it is head on with a spiritual plan of attack. We cannot do that when we isolate and allow ourselves to believe the lies of the enemy. We must combat our fears with truth.

The name of Jesus is more powerful than anything that comes against us or our children. The name of Jesus has the power to break chains and tear down strongholds. In one moment, the Holy Spirit, our helper, can take away years of pain. He leads us to our Father's heart and shows us our need for Him, gently restoring our hearts and making us new.

When we receive healing, we in turn can lead others to

healing. But we cannot operate from a place of lack and expect to be able to bring life and hope to the children within our care. As you consider the children whom God has entrusted to you, consider your position as a son or daughter of your Heavenly Father. Know that He is more than ready, willing, and able to heal the wounds within you so that you may walk in healing and lead others to His healing, too.

### Prayer

Father, I thank You for giving me the great delight and honor of caring for the children that You have entrusted to me. Sometimes I am overcome by fear, worry, and anxiety when I think about them. I do not feel adequate, and I worry that my past will prevent me from being a good enough parent to them. When these thoughts come, would you help me bring them to You? You alone are my sufficiency. When I am weak, You are strong. Sometimes parenting my children brings up things from my past, and that scares me. Help me to hide myself in You and know that You will not leave or forsake me. Help me learn to be emotionally and mentally healthy so that I can not only be an example to my children, but so that they may walk in freedom as well. Holy Spirit, show me Jesus. Help me abandon the lies for the truth and know that You are my rock, my fortress, and my deliverer. You are enough for me, and I choose to believe that Your finished work on the cross was and still is enough to cover a multitude of sins, forgive me, and reconcile me to Your heart. I believe that You have good things in store for me and my children, and I choose to entrust all of me to You today.

## Scripture to Declare

Is not this the kind of fasting I have chosen:
to loose the chains of injustice
   and untie the cords of the yoke,
to set the oppressed free
   and break every yoke?

Is it not to share your food with the hungry
   and to provide the poor wanderer with shelter—
when you see the naked, to clothe them,
   and not to turn away from your own flesh and blood?

Then your light will break forth like the dawn,
   and your healing will quickly appear;
then your righteousness will go before you,
   and the glory of the Lord will be your rear guard.

Then you will call, and the Lord will answer;
   you will cry for help, and he will say: Here am I.

If you do away with the yoke of oppression,
   with the pointing finger and malicious talk,

and if you spend yourselves in behalf of the hungry
   and satisfy the needs of the oppressed,
then your light will rise in the darkness,
   and your night will become like the noonday.

The Lord will guide you always;
   he will satisfy your needs in a sun-scorched land
   and will strengthen your frame.
You will be like a well-watered garden,
   like a spring whose waters never fail.

Your people will rebuild the ancient ruins
   and will raise up the age-old foundations;
you will be called Repairer of Broken Walls,
   Restorer of Streets with Dwellings.

    - Isaiah 58:6-12, NIV

# Day 3: Love

*Love bears all things, believes all things, hopes all things, endures all things.*
*1 Corinthians 13:7 sc ESV*

If you're a foster or adoptive parent, chances are that you have at one point believed this statement (or something like it): "With a little bit of love, these kids will be just fine!" But the truth is that many well-meaning people have opened their homes to children from hard places and then found themselves completely overwhelmed and defeated when all the love they have to give just doesn't seem to be getting them anywhere. What happens when you love with all that you have and your child still doesn't trust you? What happens when you feel like you have no love to give? What happens when you don't even like the child that is living under your roof? What happens when you just want your old life back?

As a foster parent, you are on a constant roller coaster of emotions. You are saddened by the heartbreak and trauma your child has experienced. You are angry with their family of origin for whatever happened to bring them into your care. You are prideful because you feel like you would have been a better parent for their child from the beginning. You are humbled and heartbroken for the family of origin when you realize that you could have had a story similar to theirs if a few things about your life had been different. You are constantly annoyed with your child yet simultaneously overwhelmed with a fierce sense of protection for their wellbeing.

 The beautiful thing about love is that it is not a feeling. Love is a choice. When we choose to welcome children into our homes from hard places, we actively choose to enter into heartbreak. We choose to enter into the wounds of trauma. We choose to enter into stories with darkness beyond what we will likely ever experience. Love is not a feeling. Our feelings are often fleeting. Instead, love is a choice we make, day in and day out. To wash the sheets after she has wet the bed again without complaining. To read one more story and snuggle before bed and not worry about the time on the clock. To break birth order because you know that God is telling you to say yes. To come closer when you want to walk away.

 Our Savior loved us to the point of death - not because He had an obligation to, but because He wanted to. May we also love our children from a heart of service and grace.

## Prayer

Father, thank You for the immense privilege I have of loving the children You have entrusted to me. Thank You that it is not my job to fix them. Thank you that Your love covers a multitude of sins. Your love has the power to break cycles of generational sin and to cleanse all unrighteousness from our bloodlines. Thank You for the opportunity to walk in love and exhibit love in my home. Give me a heart that is transformed by Your love. Your word says that Your perfect love casts out all fear. Cast out all fear in my heart and allow me the joy of walking with You in complete trust. Give me a love that is beyond all understanding.

I pray for supernatural bonding between my children and I. Thank You for Your promise to never leave or forsake me. Give me the courage I need to walk in the light of Your love and to trust You in all things, no matter what.

## Scripture to Declare

These things I have spoken to you, that my joy may be in you, and that your joy may be full. "This is my commandment, that you love one another as I have loved you. Greater love has no one than this, that someone lay down his life for his friends. You are my friends if you do what I command you. No longer do I call you servants, for the servant does not know what his master is doing; but I have called you friends, for all that I have heard from my Father I have made known to you. - John 15:11-15 ESV

Such love has no fear, because perfect love expels all fear. If we are afraid, it is for fear of punishment, and this shows that we have not fully experienced his perfect love. - 1 John 4:18, NLT

# Day 4: Joy

*And do not be grieved, for the joy of the Lord is your strength. - Nehemiah 8:10*

There is much to grieve when we are caring for children from hard places. We grieve the loss of innocence. We grieve the choices made that will mark their lives forever. We grieve the wounds that will need healing. But the complicated beauty of foster care is also that there is much to celebrate and thank God for. We thank God that He chose us for the honor of caring for the weak and vulnerable. We thank Him for the grace He bestows upon us each day as we lean upon His character and strength instead of resting on our own accomplishments and abilities. We thank Him for the mercies that are new each morning and for His unfailing love.

We've all heard it said that comparison is the thief of joy. But the grief of ingratitude can also steal our joy. When we look to the right or the left at our friends who seem to have it easier with their "traditional" families or seemingly perfect children, we can easily begin to forget the joys that God has set before us in the hard calling we live out each day. There are moments within this calling that seem unbearable. Our hearts are fragile as we constantly wonder what may happen when things we thought were certain turn out to be uncertain. We cry out to God, saying, "How much more? I can't give any more of myself." And yet He strengthens us to take one more step. He gives us the courage we need to do the next right thing in love.

When we look to Jesus as our source of strength and our refuge, we are filled with joy. Joy is defined as "the emotion evoked by well-being, success, or good fortune or by the prospect of possessing what one desires." When we are walking in the Spirit, our heart's desire is to be hidden in Christ. Thus, we already have what we need. Jesus never withholds Himself from us. We have the source of our joy living within us! We need not look to a spouse, children, money, or a job to satisfy us and bring us deep, abiding joy. 2 Peter 1:3 tells us that we have everything in Christ Jesus: "His divine power has granted to us all things that pertain to life and godliness, through the knowledge of him who called us to his own glory and excellence."

He is the giver of good gifts, and the greatest gift is that of Himself. We can choose joy when we choose Him. And when we choose Him, we in turn bring His joy to our homes and all who dwell within them.

### Prayer

Father, thank You for Your joy. Thank You for loving me enough to give me all of You without holding back. Help me to do the same and give all of myself to You. Thank you for giving me everything I need in You. I don't have everything I want, but I don't want to have everything that I want. I want to want You. Would you purify my desires and help me long for You above all else? Would you become the source of my joy? Help me to hide myself in You and find great joy within Your presence. I believe that You are more than enough for me and that Your love is better than life. Help me to rest in Your presence and abide in Your joy.

### Scripture to Declare

And the ransomed of the Lord shall return and come to Zion with singing; everlasting joy shall be upon their heads; they shall obtain gladness and joy, and sorrow and sighing shall flee away.
- Isaiah 35:10 ESV

A joyful heart is good medicine. - Proverbs 17:22

# Day 5: Peace

*Too long have I had my dwelling among those who hate peace. I am for peace, but when I speak, they are for war! - Psalm 120:6-7*

Oftentimes, foster care feels like a war, because it is. The work of foster care exists because there are spiritual forces at work in our world that do not want children to be safe. The enemy of our souls does not want families to live together in harmony and peace. He absolutely does not want the Lord to shine through our homes. He is diametrically opposed to the beauty of the family that God created. He thrives in chaos and confusion. But our God is a God of peace, not confusion (1 Corinthians 14:33).

The work of foster care is often frightening and unsettling. We learn of stories and realities within our communities that we wish we didn't know. Foster care forces us to come face to face with our own unsavory pasts and our glaringly obvious inadequacies. All of this can make a person want to run for cover and hide away, creating a false sense of peace by shutting out the harshness of this new world we find ourselves in. But God's peace is not a false peace. It is not a peace that exists due to the lack of strife or hardship. It is a peace that carries us and settles us in spite of and through the hardship. When everything else is falling apart, we can fall into the arms of a loving Father. Our Father holds us and comforts us in the midst of uncertainty. He reminds us of the beautiful tapestry He is weaving together. While we see the knots and gnarls of the threads that seem jumbled and messy, He sees the work of art on the other side, a masterpiece that reflects the glory of an intentional Creator.

Joseph walked through horrible trials at the hands of others - his brothers sold him into slavery, he was falsely accused by a woman and thrown into jail, his so-called buddies in jail forgot to name drop him when he got out of said jail, and he lost years of relationship with his father after being separated from his family. Yet Joseph had an unwavering confidence in the God of peace. He says in Genesis 50:20, "You intended to harm me, but God intended it all for good. He brought me to this position so I could save the lives of many people."

Oftentimes, the very situations in our lives that have threatened to rob us of our peace, joy, and confidence are the very basis for which God will found our ministry. Scripture tells us that we are comforted so that we can comfort others. (2 Corinthians 1:3-5) The hard parts of our stories (and our children's) - abuse, trauma, betrayal, loneliness - all of these things are what God can use to bring light and hope to one another. The world around us is scary and heavy. But God sent His Son to earth as the Prince of Peace. The beautiful gift of Jesus' life on earth is that He didn't leave us alone. He gave us the third person of the Trinity - the Holy Spirit - to dwell within us as our Counselor and Helper. So when you feel that peace is nowhere to be found, you only have to look within to find the same power that raised Christ Jesus from the dead dwelling in you and empowering you to walk in peace that can only come from Him.

## Prayer

Father, it is so easy for me to feel overwhelmed and frightened. Oftentimes peace feels far away, because my life can seem anything but peaceful. I want to know Your peace. I want to rest in You and find my confidence in You alone. I know that You alone are the source of peace. This peace strengthens me and gives me exactly what I need to be able to walk with You and do what You have called me to do. Help me to run to You and not be afraid to admit when I need Your peace to take over my heart. I need You, Father. Fill me anew with Your Spirit, and help me to be a carrier of peace to others.

## Scripture to Declare

I have said these things to you, that in me you may have peace. In the world you will have tribulation. But take heart; I have overcome the world. - John 16:33

You keep him in perfect peace whose mind is stayed on you, because he trusts in you. Trust in the Lord forever, for the Lord God is an everlasting rock. - Isaiah 26:3-4

The Lord sits enthroned over the flood; the Lord sits enthroned as king forever. May the Lord give strength to his people! May the Lord bless his people with peace! - Psalm 29:10-11

# Day 6: Patience

*Be patient, therefore, brothers, until the coming of the Lord. See how the farmer waits for the precious fruit of the earth, being patient about it, until it receives the early and the late rains. - James 5:7*

There is a reason why a synonym for patience is "longsuffering." There is a reason why people say, "Don't pray for patience; you'll get what you ask for!" Patience, or long-suffering, is a fruit of the Spirit that is hard for us to grapple with in today's instant culture. Amazon Prime can get us our order in one day. Target has a drive up service that has orders ready in two hours. Instacart can get us groceries in an hour. How have we allowed our waiting muscles to atrophy so much?

A dear friend of mine once explained the difference between healing and a miracle. She said that a miracle is often an instantaneous happening in which something is completely changed. For instance, a person with cancer no longer has cancer. But healing is different; it is a process. And the process of healing hurts. As foster parents, we say that we want our children to enter into healing when they become a part of our families. But oftentimes, what we want is a miracle. We want them to be healed overnight. We do not want to sound like a broken record when we are constantly redirecting or sharing the same truths with them. We do not want to endure the arduous process of planting, watering, and then harvesting the seeds. We want to plant the seed one day and see the fruit the next day.

But the biblical law of the harvest says that when we plant the seeds, we will reap a harvest if we do not give up. (Galatians 6:9) The time spent watering seeds and tending to the plants that grow by pruning them is not an easy or overnight process. The gardener spends his time pruning plants back in order that they might grow and produce more fruit. So it is with our children. We speak words of life over them, knowing that one day, we will reap a harvest and see them walk in the identity that is theirs in Christ. We encourage them when they cannot encourage themselves, knowing that God is doing something beautiful in their hearts, even when we cannot see it. We pray over them and entrust them to God over and over again, knowing that He who began a good work in them will be faithful to complete it (Phil 1). The best fruit will come when we wait for it. No one wants to eat unripe fruit. The same is true for our children. God will work in them, and we cannot rush the process He has already begun in their lives.

**Prayer**

Father, sometimes my children behave in ways that make me feel crazy! I am so easily annoyed, and I know that is my flesh, not my spirit. I know that You have entrusted my children to me so that they may know You and encounter Your love. They cannot encounter Your love through me if I am constantly nagging or focusing on all the things they do wrong. They cannot encounter Your love through me if I am in a perpetually bad mood because I am overwhelmed and not relying on Your strength. So Father, I ask you to empower me. Fill me anew with Your Spirit, Who is patience embodied. Help me know how to trust You in the process. You have done so much in my life and have changed me from the inside out. This took time, and there are people who were patient with me when my edges were much more rough. Now I need to be that person in my child's life. Enable me to walk in patience so that I see the beautiful work You are doing and rejoice every step of the way.

**Scripture to Declare**

Blessed is the man who remains steadfast under trial, for when he has stood the test he will receive the crown of life, which God has promised to those who love him. - James 1:12

As for that in the good soil, they are those who, hearing the word, hold it fast in an honest and good heart, and bear fruit with patience. - Luke 8:15

You also, be patient. Establish your hearts, for the coming of the Lord is at hand. - James 5:8

# Day 7: Kindness

*From the same mouth come blessing and cursing. My brothers, these things ought not to be so. - James 3:10*

"Is it true? Is it necessary? Is it kind?" These are the questions that Dr. Emerson Eggerichs says should precede our speech.[1] We often speak without thinking or acknowledging the power of our words. We do not think about how our words can either tear up or build down. It is much easier for us to tear someone down with a sarcastic comment or a nasty judgement. Why is it so much more difficult to speak an intentional word of encouragement to someone? Why do we struggle to speak with kindness to those we love the most?

Maybe our hearts are insecure. The ones we love the most are the people who are living within our homes, and unfortunately, they can see our faults. They know when we are not walking the walk and are merely talking the talk. Proverbs tells us that life and death are in

---

[1] That Sounds Fun Podcast Episode 60: Dr. Emerson Eggerichs [Interview by 947744841 739530945 A. F. Downs]. (2017, November 9).

the power of the tongue. (Proverbs 18:21) We often do not live like that is true. We do not speak as though the lives of those around us depend on our words. When our hearts are not rooted in the perfect love of Christ, what flows out of our mouths reflects our insecurities. Instead of building others up, we tear people down because what we feel inside is not good.

Kindness is "the quality of being friendly, generous, and considerate." Being nice, on the other hand is being "pleasant, agreeable, and satisfactory." Being nice is "going along to get along." It is the status quo of being a generally agreeable person. But kindness goes the extra mile. Kindness is staying up late to help with the math homework even when your child procrastinated or has a bad attitude. Kindness is extending forgiveness and choosing to connect when you want to punish out of anger.

God demonstrated the ultimate kindness to us in sending His Son to save us. He chooses to exhibit His kindness to us over and over when He is slow to anger as we deal with the same sins over and over again. He chooses to be kind to us when we cannot even be kind to ourselves. The Word says that His kindness leads us to repentance. If we want to see our children's hearts change, we will need to be kind. We cannot go wrong when we lead with kindness.

**Prayer**

Father, I admit that sometimes I do not want to be kind. Sometimes I would rather be right. I want to prove a point and feel justified in my actions. But I know there is a better way. I know that You want me to be kind so that my children can see Your love more clearly and can more easily receive from You. I know that You are a kind Father who longs to love and give generously to His children. I pray You help me to see Your kindness in my life so that I can give it away to my children. I want them to know Your kindness and model repentance for them so that they know what it means to walk with You.

**Scripture to Declare**

She opens her mouth with wisdom, and the teaching of kindness is on her tongue. - Proverbs 31:26

He has told you, O man, what is good; and what does the Lord require of you but to do justice, and to love kindness, and to walk humbly with your God? - Micah 6:8

# Day 8: Goodness

*I remain confident of this: I will see the goodness of the Lord in the land of the living. - Psalm 27:13*

What comes to mind when you think about goodness? Chances are your mind floods with images that bring a smile to your face and levity to your heart. You most likely choose to dwell on things that bring happiness and joy. But the thing about God is that His ways are not our ways, and His thoughts are not our thoughts. So what is good to Him may not feel particularly good to us.

*I used to take my health and my presumed ability to procreate for granted. It seemed pretty easy for most people around me to make babies, so I figured it would be the same for me. That hasn't been the case so far. And you know what? It sucks. It really, really sucks.*

*But this is what I know. There is no pain like that of an empty womb. Nothing. It is the deepest and most raw pain I have ever felt. This summer I found myself sitting on the floor of our living room shaking and crying my eyes out and saying to my husband, "Nothing will make this pain go away. No matter how hard I try to busy myself with other things and enjoy other things about my life, this pain still lingers. It hurts and it won't go away and I don't know what to do. I know I have a great life. I love you. I love our house. I love our friends. But I don't have a baby and I don't know when we will have a baby and it hurts so bad."*

I wrote those words nearly three years ago in the midst of an unexpected and unwelcome infertility journey. It didn't feel good to me when we tried to conceive for almost two years while countless friends had babies without a second thought. But God - He can make something out of nothing. He brings beauty from ashes. Now I sit on the other side of that journey, thanking God for His goodness in the midst of it and knowing that all along, He was with me. He knew that ultimately, His goodness would shine through my story.

If I had conceived on my timeline, my husband and I likely would not have pursued foster care at the time we did. If I had conceived in my time, my daughter would not be my daughter, and I cannot imagine my life without her. How I shudder to think of all the good things in my life that I would not have if God had eradicated the hard things that I wanted to be rid of!

Katherine Wolf says in *Suffer Strong*, "God made you to do the hard thing in the good story He's writing for your life."[2] It doesn't feel good to learn about the dark history that our kids walked through before coming to our home. It doesn't feel good to walk through trials that take our breath away and leave us spinning and fearful. But good things and hard things can coexist, and God can completely change our perspective to allow us to see how He is working on our behalf, even in situations that feel hopeless.

---

[2] Wolf, K. (2020). Hope Heals : Katherine Wolf // Jay Wolf Instagram Story Quotes Highlight. Retrieved September 26, 2020, from https://www.instagram.com/hopeheals/

My sweet friend Gretchen often talks about putting on our "Gospel glasses" in order to see the world through God's eyes.[3] We cannot give thanks for the hard things and see God's goodness if our eyes are focused on our circumstances. We have to look up to see Him. And when we do, we will see that He is working all things together for our good and for His glory.

---

[3] Saffles, G. (2018, May 08). Gospel Glasses – Well-Watered Women. Retrieved September 26, 2020, from https://wellwateredwomen.com/gospel-glasses/

**Prayer**

Father, I want to see as You see. I want to think as You do. Rid me of the thought that Your love is only good when I feel good. I know that Your goodness reaches to the depths of my hurt and pain and that You do the same for my children. When things are hard, I want to praise You. When things are easy, I want to praise You. Help me to praise You no matter how hard or easy my days are. I want to come to You with everything in my life, knowing that You are a God of abundance and goodness. Help me to believe this and model it for my children to see that they can trust You, too.

**Scripture to Declare**

Moses said, "Please show me your glory." And he said, "I will make all my goodness pass before you and will proclaim before you my name 'The Lord.' And I will be gracious to whom I will be gracious, and will show mercy on whom I will show mercy."
- Exodus 33:18-19

Blessed is the one you choose and bring near, to dwell in your courts! We shall be satisfied with the goodness of your house, the holiness of your temple! - Psalm 65:4

# Day 9: Gentleness

*Pursue righteousness, godliness, faith, love, steadfastness, gentleness. - 1 Timothy 6:11*

When my husband and I were dating, I was struck by his kind personality. He had a way of bringing calm and peace to my hurried and frenzied life. Looking back, I can see that it was his gentleness that won my heart. As a social butterfly, before I met my husband I was often attracted to men who were just like me—loud, gregarious, life of the party. But this man with his quiet and steadfast spirit? I didn't quite know what to do with him.

Gentleness is "the quality of being kind, tender, or mild-mannered." This is my husband personified. I used to believe that gentleness or meekness was a sign of weakness. I did not know that in order to be gentle, you were actually practicing the art of self-control through reigning in and managing great strength. I was accustomed to forcing my way and manipulating situations to make sure I got my way. But this new way of living—to be open, honest, and still be loved—this was all at once terrifying and freeing.

Our children have come from places in which they did not have a voice. Their stories hold years of pain that is far beyond anything we would wish upon our worst enemy. In our good intentions, we may want to sweep into their lives and change everything right away, looking for a place where we can act as a savior that brings hope and healing. But we were never meant to save our children. We are only meant to love them. The only thing we can do as foster parents is to love with a humble gentleness. The smallest things are what make a difference in the lives of our children. I remember when our daughter first came to live with us, she would say "thank you" after every meal together. It was precious and a reminder of the things that we often take for granted.

I don't know about you, but I often am quick to see the faults in people. This doesn't always come from a critical spirit, but rather from a desire for things to be right. When our children come into our lives, there can often be a temptation to fix them. We see all that has gone wrong in their lives, and we desperately want to make it right, starting with us. But God does not expect us to fix them. He does not expect us to get it right all the time. He simply asks us to love with gentleness. To be a safe place for them to land. To encourage them and hold them and be present as a person who cares. After all, it only takes one caring person to change someone's life forever. Maybe God will allow us to be that person for our children.

**Prayer**

Father, it would be easy for me to try to make grand sweeping changes in my child's life, because I see all that has gone wrong, and I want to fix it. I want to take the pain away from them, and I want it to be gone now. But in my life, I have seen that change and growth take time. You have brought change to my life, but You did so in such a kind and gentle way. Your gentleness drew me to You and helped me know that I could trust You with everything. Father, help me to be a gentle parent who leads with love and kindness. Help me to know that Your love covers a multitude of sins, including my own. Help my child to see Your love through me and be drawn to Your love as You shine through my brokenness.

**Scripture to Declare**

I therefore, a prisoner for the Lord, urge you to walk in a manner worthy of the calling to which you have been called, with all humility and gentleness, with patience, bearing with one another in love, eager to maintain the unity of the Spirit in the bond of peace.- Ephesians 4:1-3

Brothers, if anyone is caught in any transgression, you who are spiritual should restore him in a spirit of gentleness. Keep watch on yourself, lest you too be tempted. Bear one another's burdens, and so fulfill the law of Christ. For if anyone thinks he is something, when he is nothing, he deceives himself. - Galatians 6:1-3

# Day 10: Faithfulness

*You turn mourning to dancing*
*You give beauty for ashes*
*You turn shame into glory*
*You're the only one who can*

*You turn graves into garden*
*You turn bones into armies*
*You turn seas into highways*
*You're the only one who can*

*"Graves to Gardens" by Elevation Worship*

I remember sitting in a staff meeting at the school where I was teaching as a fresh-faced college graduate in Chihuahua, Mexico. A fellow staff member was sharing about what God was teaching him, and he said, "Whenever I forget the faithfulness of God, I just look back at His track record. It's 100%." That has stuck with me in so many times of uncertainty. As someone who loves to plan and enjoys forward thinking about the future, it is easy for me to think that I can control everything if I just maintain enough organization and strategy, things will go exactly the way I want them to go. But that is just not the case. Life is full of surprises, some of them exciting, and some of them heartbreaking.

When I think about all that God has done in my life, I can say with confidence that He has been faithful. I can look back and trace His hand through situations that in the moment seemed insurmountable and impossible. But God. He came through and He changed everything in ways that only He can. The song lyrics above paint a picture of a God who is faithful to do what He says He will do. He takes our ordinary lives and turns them into something extraordinary.

When we look at the Israelites in the Old Testament, we see a people who are often faithless. The Israelite people were enslaved by the Egyptians for 400 years, and when God called Moses to lead them out, they went out with dancing and praise, walking on dry land through the Red Sea as their enemies were defeated. But when they reached the other side and the journey proved difficult, their complaints for the life they knew before were quick to follow. I've heard it said that "a known hell is more comfortable than the unknown paradise." The Israelites looked back on their days in Egypt with rose-colored glasses. As soon as things were difficult in their new life, they wanted to go back to what they knew, even though it was full of oppression and opposition. God had made a promise to the Israelites through Abraham, and they knew that He was going to bless them and multiply their people. But when they fixed their eyes on their lack, they became forgetful and lost their hope in the One who brought them out of Egypt.

As I read through the story of Moses in Exodus, one of my study Bibles notes that Moses was a foster child. All of a sudden, my eyes were opened to see how God's great plan touches not only those who have great families and come from safe places, but those whose beginning in life was less than ideal. Moses was spared by the Hebrew midwives and brought to the river in faith by a mother who loved him too much to sacrifice him in obedience to an evil pharaoh. God allowed this pharaoh's daughter to draw Moses from the water and raised him to a place of influence.

God's plans for us are good. His plans for our children are good. It is easy for us to take a look at difficult circumstances and lose heart by thinking of all the things that are lacking and that need to be changed. But God looks at broken circumstances and is not afraid of them or turned away. He sees the beauty and the potential for His glory. And He is the One who is faithful to redeem us.

## Prayer

Father, thank You for Your faithfulness. Thank You that You are the One who can make something out of nothing. Thank You for Your kindness in bringing my children to me. I am not able to change their future, but You can. I ask that You help me to show them how to trace Your hand of faithfulness in their lives. Help me show them how to see Your beauty and grace in the midst of fear and uncertainty. Help me hold on to hope for them when they cannot do it for themselves. Thank You for being faithful, even when I am faithless.

## Scripture to Declare

The Lord descended in the cloud and stood with him there, and proclaimed the name of the Lord. The Lord passed before him and proclaimed, "The Lord, the Lord, a God merciful and gracious, slow to anger, and abounding in steadfast love and faithfulness, keeping steadfast love for thousands, forgiving iniquity and transgression and sin, but who will by no means clear the guilty, visiting the iniquity of the fathers on the children and the children's children, to the third and the fourth generation." - Exodus 34:5-7

I will make with them an everlasting covenant, that I will not turn away from doing good to them. And I will put the fear of me in their hearts, that they may not turn from me. I will rejoice in doing them good, and I will plant them in this land in faithfulness, with all my heart and all my soul. - Jeremiah 32:40-41

# Day 11: Self-Control

*A man without self-control is like a city broken into and left without walls. - Proverbs 25:28*

When we began our training to become foster parents, we learned about the importance of teaching our children to regulate. In a sense, we are helping them learn how to respond to the world around them by teaching them not to allow their feelings to completely control them. Chuck Swindoll wisely said, "I am convinced that life is 10% what happens to me and 90% how I react to it."

Think about your own life, and then think about the stories you know that children from hard places carry. Oftentimes, our knee-jerk reaction to difficult circumstances is not to find rest and peace in the arms of our Savior. When left to our own devices, we are prone to depression, anxiety, and fear. But in order to help our children find healthy rhythms, we must take steps to remind ourselves of God's truth when things are hard and surround ourselves with others who will do the same for us. Imagine how much more our children need the same. Our children have not had people speaking truth into their lives. They have not had people telling them that there is another way. So we must be that voice.

Self-control is not only characterized by what we avoid, but also by the intentional choices we make. When I am acting out of my own insecurities, I often lash out at the ones closest to me—my husband and my kids. My words are harsh and cold instead of gentle and kind. Self-control shows up when I take the first steps toward reconciliation by apologizing and asking for forgiveness. Just yesterday I had to ask my teenage daughter for a fresh start after snapping at her. Our kids need humble parents who are willing to acknowledge their flaws. By showing our children how to take ownership of your faults, we can help them understand the value of serving others within relationship and the beauty of living within a family that seeks to love one another well.

**Prayer**

Father, sometimes it is easy for me to forget the dark and sad history that my children have faced before coming into my home. Other times, it seems as though their history is all that I can see when I look at them. Help me to see them the way You do. I don't want to view them with deficits. I want to see in the Spirit. Help me to call forth good things in them and to speak the truth in love. Help me show them how to respond to difficulties and trials with faith instead of fear. Help me teach them how to trust You and know Your goodness. Help me walk with You and control my emotions so that they can learn to do the same.

**Scripture to Declare**

Do you not know that in a race all the runners run, but only one receives the prize? So run that you may obtain it. Every athlete exercises self-control in all things. They do it to receive a perishable wreath, but we an imperishable. - 1 Corinthians 9:24-25

For this very reason, make every effort to supplement your faith with virtue, and virtue with knowledge, and knowledge with self-control, and self-control with steadfastness, and steadfastness with godliness, and godliness with brotherly affection, and brotherly affection with love. - 2 Peter 1:5-7

# Day 12: Hope

*But this I call to mind, and therefore I have hope: The steadfast love of the Lord never ceases; his mercies never come to an end; they are new every morning; great is your faithfulness.*

*- Lamentations 3:22-23*

When our circumstances are difficult, hope can be the last thing we feel we have in abundance. But hope is the very thing that can help us keep going in the midst of the impossible. Think about the Israelites. God made a covenant vow with Abraham, their patriarch, to make him a fruitful nation that would be an example to everyone around them. He said that He would make his descendants as numerous as the stars in the sky. Hundreds of years later, God speaks to Moses from the burning bush and tells him that it is time for the Israelites to be free. Moses has many times of doubt and fear, but overall, he is a man who trusts God to help lead the Israelites from captivity to freedom. The Israelites are a fickle and frail people, much like us. They question and wander and rebel, and when Moses loses his patience with them one too many times, he loses his privilege to enter the Promised Land.

What do you think it was that kept Moses going when the Israelites whined and complained about the manna or began to worship a golden calf? Was it his hope in their ability to get it together? I highly doubt it. It seems Moses' hope was rooted in the unchanging character of God. Friends, the same can be true for us. We may survey the circumstances of our children's lives (or our own lives!) and see a hopeless horizon. It may feel as though there is absolutely nothing that we can praise God for or see as a bright light in the midst of the darkness. We may be walking through the wilderness and feel as though the streams of refreshing are nowhere to be found. But God is the Author of our stories, and He is not done yet. We are in the middle of a grand narrative with twists and turns, but the wonderful thing is that we know the ending—He wins! The enemy of our souls will not have the final word.

So when you get a call from the school about your child's behavior, or you have a difficult court hearing, or you just feel like running away from home because it all seems to be too much, remember this—He who calls you is faithful, and He will surely do it (1 Thessalonians 5:24). He will surely bring you to a place of peace when you surrender to Him. He will surely make your hope rise when you feel like you can barely keep your head above water. He will surely supply all of your needs according to His riches in glory in Christ Jesus. (Philippians 4:19) He. Will. Do. It.

**Prayer**

Father, when I look at my situation, it just feels hopeless. I am having a hard time seeing anything positive in the midst of the disheartening. But I know that You are greater. It is easy to look at the circumstances and see nothing but a sad future ahead. But I know that You are greater. Help me to place my hope in You. I do not want to place my hope in my circumstances, because I know that they can change and will not ultimately satisfy me. Help me to know that Your grace is sufficient for me, for Your power is made perfect in my weakness. In my weakness, I am admitting to You that I cannot see the light. But I want to see it, so train my eyes to see the hope that You have placed in the midst of my life.

**Scripture to Declare**

Though the fig tree should not blossom, nor fruit be on the vines, the produce of the olive fail and the fields yield no food, the flock be cut off from m the fold and there be no herd in the stalls, yet I will rejoice in the LORD; I will take joy in the God of my salvation. GOD, the Lord, is my strength; He makes my feet like the deer's; He makes me tread on my high places. - Habakkuk 3:17-19

May the God of hope fill you with all joy and peace in believing, so that by the power of the Holy Spirit you may abound in love. - Romans 15:13

# Day 13: Physical Health

*So whether you eat or drink or whatever you do, do it all for the glory of God. - 1 Corinthians 10:31*

We all know the things we are supposed to do to take care of ourselves— *eat those veggies, get enough sleep, and get some exercise, for crying out loud!* But how do we make time for these things when we are living in survival mode? I know what you're thinking - this is a book about prayer. Why are we talking about health and wellness? Well, friend, our spiritual, emotional, physical, and mental health are all wrapped up with one another. If you are a licensed foster parent, you most likely have had some type of trauma training in which you learned about how to help your kids regulate. And most likely, you learned about how physical activity is an important part of the regulation process. Our children have been through horrific events that have changed the way their brains function, and we are working to reverse these changes by offering a safe place for them to find healing. Our hope is that they find healing in the person of Jesus Christ.

But how can we help them if we do not know how to take care of ourselves? Research has emerged that shows us the importance of using both sides of our brain in order to help us process and heal from traumatic events. EMDR is a special type of therapy that has been used to help people heal and begin to build new pathways in their brains from past traumas in order to move forward. This therapy uses bilateral stimulation to reprocess events, but it doesn't take a highly specialized therapist to use bilateral stimulation. The beauty of bilateral stimulation is that some form of it is available to all of us at little to no cost. All we have to do is lace up our walking shoes and hit the pavement.

Studies have shown that walking is good for your health because it can help weight loss, but did you know that walking is also highly beneficial for your mental health? Walking can:

1. Lower your risk of depression

2. Improve your overall cognitive functioning

3. Release endorphins

4. Release the protein BDNF, which improves brain health

5. Help with mental and physical fatigue

6. Strengthen your hippocampus, the part of the brain that processes and stores memories

7. Improve creativity

8. Increase blood flow in your brain[4]

---

[4] Rodriguez-Cayro, K. (2018, August 16). 8 Ways Walking Changes Your Brain For The Better, According To Science. Retrieved September 26, 2020, from https://www.bustle.com/p/8-ways-walking-changes-your-brain-for-the-better-according-to-science-10077769

Still not convinced? Just 2 hours of walking per week — equivalent to around 17 minutes per day — has been shown to lower the risk of premature death.[5] We all want to live long and fruitful lives on this earth. We want to see our children grow up and be around to take care of our grandchildren. But we cannot do that if we completely ignore our physical health. If we want to be emotionally, mentally, and spiritually well, we cannot ignore our physical lives.

God instructs us to take care of our bodies because they are a temple for His Holy Spirit. A temple is a dwelling place. It is where the people of God come to meet with Him. We are blessed to have the Holy Spirit dwelling within us because of the beautiful sacrifice of our Savior, Jesus Christ. When we choose to honor our bodies by sleeping enough, getting exercise, and eating for energy instead of out of boredom or to hide and stuff emotions, we choose to honor God and show up for our children. We give our children the best of ourselves when we choose to take care of ourselves.

Choosing to get outside and go for a walk as a family brings connection.[6] When our kids are too afraid to look us in the eyes and too wound up to sit down and focus on their school work, we can take a walk. When we are so stressed that we can feel our emotions right under our skin, we can take a walk. It doesn't have to be hours long—just start small. I've found that ten minutes back and forth up the block have been beneficial to me when I needed to clear my head. Getting enough sleep improves our thought processes and allows us the cognition we need to respond in love instead of reacting in anger

---

[5] Merle, A. (2018, November 02). Walking Can Save Your Life. Retrieved September 26, 2020, from https://medium.com/@andrewmerle/walking-can-save-your-life-21b7997dc636

[6] Lavelle, C. (2019, June 17). 8 reasons you're right to insist on a family walk. Retrieved September 26, 2020, from https://www.netdoctor.co.uk/healthy-living/wellbeing/a27430/health-benefits-of-family-walk/

or fear to our children's behaviors. Eating well helps us feel well and fuels us to make better decisions throughout the day. So today, take a step toward physical wellness. Your body and your children will thank you.

**Prayer**

Father, I know that I need to take care of my physical health, but sometimes I am just so overwhelmed with getting through the day that I don't feel like I have any energy left to pay attention to taking care of my body. I know that I only have one body, and that it is important for me to care for it. Help me to take steps to care for my body so that I can continue to care for the people You have given to me to shepherd. I know that You want me to function at my best, and I need Your help so that I can love them well. Physical health will enable me to care for them with energy and strength.

**Scripture to Declare**

Or do you not know that your body is a temple of the Holy Spirit within you, whom you have from God? You are not your own, for you were bought with a price. So glorify God in your body. - 1 Corinthians 6:19-20

She dresses herself with strength and makes her arms strong. - Proverbs 31:17

Rather train yourself for godliness; for while bodily training is of some value, godliness is of value in every way, as it holds promise for the present life and also for the life to come. - 1 Timothy 4:7-8

# Day 14: Marriage

*Therefore a man shall leave his father and his mother and hold fast to his wife, and they shall become one flesh. - Genesis 2:24*

When you stand before your spouse on your wedding day, you make promises to fully love someone whom you do not fully know. You think that you have been through some things with them, but nothing really prepares you for what life is like when you mold two people together as one. If you are married, you know that to some degree, rose-colored glasses influence your dating and engaged life. Try as you may, there is an element to showing only your best to your spouse-to-be before the vows are said. When the honeymoon is over (or maybe during the honeymoon), there is a realization of what has happened. You are stuck with this person. Forever.

I don't know about you, but marriage was a pretty rude awakening for me. My life prior to marriage was one in which I performed and earned the approval of others through my accomplishments and hard work ethic. In my mind, there were certain things that "good Christian girls" did and did not do. My idea of what it meant to love and be loved by my Heavenly Father was so skewed. As a young child, I accepted Christ. But it wasn't until my mid-twenties that I truly began to understand my identity in Him. He hadn't saved me and called me by name just so that I could be a good little soldier for Him. He wanted to know me and be known by me.

Marriage was a context in which my relationship with the Lord began to flourish, because I saw my weakness and my sin on display. This incredible man I had prayed and longed for was standing in front of me, longing to love me, and yet my fears and insecurities often pushed him away instead of drawing him closer. We can now laugh at the early days of miscommunication and hot tempers, but it has taken time for us to find a healthy rhythm of communication.

In marriage, there are tremendous highs and deep lows. The same can be said about any relationship, but our marriage should be the most important relationship in our lives, second only to our relationship with our Heavenly Father. When we welcome children from hard places into our homes, chances are that they have not seen a healthy marriage on display. Our unique opportunity to show them what marriage can be is such a great calling, and a huge responsibility.

When people look at your marriage, do they see Christ? Does your marriage push people toward Jesus? Christ is the head of the church, just as the husband is the head of the home and the family. Is your marriage a picture of the bride and bridegroom of Christ, loving and serving one another? Or is it a place of great tension and turmoil? In order to serve our kids well, we must invest in our marriages. This investment will look different in each season, but God will reward us for the time we spend together, and our children will be better for it as well.

Our marriage is the foundation of our home. We are built upon Christ, and He upholds us so that we can uphold our children. If our marriage is shaky, the whole home struggles under the weight of our sin. But if we are loving one another well and exhibiting the love of Christ, our children will see the love of God in a whole new light.

### Prayer

Father, thank You for my spouse. Thank You for the way You created him/her in Your image and knit him/her together with great intention. I thank You for our differences and that we can complement each other with our strengths and weaknesses. Sometimes I see his/her differences as a bother to me instead of a blessing. Help me to see that our differences are what help us present a whole and united front to our children. Help us pick up our crosses daily and love each other well so that they know what it means to love with intentionality and kindness. Please provide good caretakers for our children so that we can enjoy time away together. Help me to remember the early days and dwell on all the qualities that attracted me to my spouse instead of trying to fix him/her. Thank you for the gift that he/she is in my life. May I never take him/her for granted.

### Scripture to Declare

Let love be genuine. Abhor what is evil; hold fast to what is good. Love one another with brotherly affection. Outdo one another in showing honor. - Romans 12:9-10

However, let each one of you love his wife as himself, and let the wife see that she respects her husband. - Ephesians 5:33

I am my beloved's, and his desire is for me. - Song of Solomon 7:10

# Day 15: Biological Children

*Behold, children are a heritage from the Lord,*

*the fruit of the womb a reward. - Psalm 127:3*

When we became foster parents, we did not have biological children. We were also in the midst of a season of infertility. Many people assumed that we were becoming foster parents because we could not have children. This assumption was false and hurtful for many reasons. Children in care are not a second choice or a placeholder. They are not objects that are discarded or tossed about without thought. They are made in the image of God, and they are human beings with needs and desires, just like us. Our desire to become foster parents was based on a calling from God.

There is much debate about whether to foster if you have biological children, whether or not you should break birth order, how many children you "should" have in your home at any given time, and what is considered "normal" or "acceptable." Our first placement was extremely difficult and somewhat shell-shocking. After this placement, we took a much needed break, and I miraculously got pregnant after almost two years of trying to conceive. We had always said that if I were to get pregnant while we had children in our home, we would continue fostering them. A new addition to the family did not mean that the children in our care had to find a new place to live!

When I got pregnant after the children had left, the fears began to creep in. How in the world could we continue to foster when I had this new life growing within me? I had never been a biological mom before and cared for a newborn. I knew nothing of the sleepless nights and the long days that were physically demanding. Everything within me began to wonder if we should reconsider the plan to continue fostering and push it off until I felt more comfortable with the idea.

But God in His great mercy and kindness helped me remember why we said yes to fostering in the first place. It wasn't out of a love for comfort and security. It was through a desire to bring comfort and security to those who do not have it. It was because we couldn't unlearn what we knew to be true - that the crisis in our state meant that kids all over the place are being shipped off to different counties, group homes, and institutions because people simply are not stepping up to take care of them. And so I knew that even though it would be scary, we had to keep going.

Our biological children are our forever babies. We love and cherish them and know them from the inside out, because they were formed within. How we long to know our children in care in this same way. Outsiders looking in may question us, and our own doubts and fears may haunt us, too. What if our biological kids are traumatized by the behaviors of our kids from hard places? What if our bio kids are afraid? What if our bio kids cannot understand the loss and the transition when kids in care shuffle in and out of our home?

All of these questions are worth asking, and we all have to make the decision that is best for our family. But they are not too hard for our God. The beauty of foster care is that every family will look different, but every family will be stitched together by God. We can entrust our bio kids to God, knowing that He will use the ministry of foster care to shape and mold them into who He has created them to be.

**Prayer**

Father, sometimes I am afraid for my biological children. I wonder if fostering does more harm than good. It is a lot to ask of a child, and I don't want them to resent me for pulling them into our calling when they grow up. But I also know that You say that children are a blessing. I believe that is true for biological, foster, and adopted children. Help us to create a life-giving home that encourages our bio children to live lives of kindness, generosity, boldness, and courage. Help them to know that they are loved. Help them to learn to love sacrificially, and help them learn to empathize and come alongside those who need the love of the Father.

**Scripture to Declare**

And these words that I command you today shall be on your heart. You shall teach them diligently to your children, and shall talk of them when you sit in your house, and when you walk by the way, and when you lie down, and when you rise. - Deuteronomy 6:6-7

He has told you, O man, what is good; and what does the Lord require of you but to do justice, and to love kindness and to walk humbly with your God? - Micah 6:8

Now they were bringing even infants to him that he might touch them. And when the disciples saw it, they rebuked them. But Jesus called them to him, saying, "Let the children come to me, and do not hinder them, for to such belongs the kingdom of God. - Luke 18:15-16

# Day 16: Children in Care

*Father of the fatherless and protector of widows is God in his holy habitation. - Psalm 68:5*

  Chances are, if you are reading this book, it is because you felt a tug on your heart to become a foster parent. And that tug on your heart was most likely a whisper (or a yell) from the Holy Spirit. It is easy to know about a "cause" and feel sympathetic to those who are suffering. But when you learn of the foster care crisis and see the faces of vulnerable children, everything changes. To get a call and hear the horrific details of what children have endured brings clarity to what it means to suffer.

  When a child enters our home, we have high hopes. We want to show them how to live life tethered to Christ. We want generational bonds to be broken in order for families to reunify. We want so much for our children, and yet we often find ourselves disappointed because reality does not live up to our dreams. Even for the most experienced foster parent, expectations can remain unmet as we encounter the realities of everyday life in the midst of unpacking trauma.

One of the most important things I have heard as a foster parent is this truth: "Our children are not our ministry." They are not our projects. They are simply our children—human beings who have emotional, physical, and mental needs. We are extremely limited in what we can give our children. We did not have the experience of preparing for their arrival for nine months as we would with a biological child. They come to us in nontraditional ways, but for the time allotted by God, they are ours. And while they are ours, we are to love them. With everything that we have, we are to give them the unconditional love of a Father Who never changes or casts a shifting shadow. When no one else has been trustworthy, we are to prove ourselves trustworthy so they know that their Heavenly Father is trustworthy and true. When everyone else walks away, we come closer so they know the nearness of a God who never leaves or forsakes His children.

The temptation to pull away in the midst of difficult behaviors, complicated family dynamics, and frustrating requirements is real. But God is greater than all of these. Nothing is impossible for Him. Oftentimes, in the midst of hard situations, we say, "The only thing I can do is pray" as if prayer is a last resort. We treat prayer as an option for what we do when we've tried everything else, but it should be the other way around. Prayer needs to be our first line of defense against the enemy's schemes and plans for our lives. Prayer changes us. Corrie Ten Boom was a Christian woman who fearlessly hid Jews from the Nazis during World War II. She wisely asked, "Is prayer your steering wheel or your spare tire?"

As we seek to parent children from hard places (or any child for that matter), we are faced with our insecurities and our weaknesses. Our natural inclination is to find a way to fix these things. But our God has given us everything we need, if only we come to Him. Let us commit to pray for children in care, knowing that God alone will change their hearts and lives in His perfect timing and His perfect way.

## Prayer

Father, I admit that I do not pray for my children as often as I would like to. I know the power of prayer, but I am often too prideful to come to You when I need You. I want to be seen as resourceful and able to "handle it all." But I know the power of the Gospel is made perfect in my weakness. God, I admit that I am weak. I do not know how to handle all of the history that my children have brought into my home. In my selfishness, I wish I could wave a magic wand and make it all go away. But I know that there is beauty in the brokenness, and your word says that You are always doing a new thing (Isaiah 43:18) Lord, would You do a new thing in me? I know that as You change my heart, You will help me to respond in love when I would normally react in fear. I pray for my children and ask that You change them from the inside out. Help them to love You with all of their heart, soul, mind, and strength. Give them a teachable heart that longs to know You. Thank You for the gift of being a part of their life, even if only for a season.

## Scripture to Declare

For as the rain and the snow come down from heaven and do not return there but water the earth, making it bring forth and sprout, giving seed to the sower and bread to the eater, so shall my word be that goes out from my mouth; it shall not return to me empty, but it shall accomplish that which I purpose, and shall succeed in the thing for which I sent it. -Isaiah   55:10-11

Now the parable is this: The seed is the word of God.

As for that in the good soil, they are those who, hearing the word, hold it fast in an honest and good heart, and bear fruit with patience. - Luke   8:11, 15

# Day 17: Biological Parents

*My brothers, show no partiality as you hold the faith in our Lord Jesus Christ, the Lord of glory. - James 2:1*

Whether you choose to admit it or not, pride plays a role in the attitude you may have toward your child's biological parents. After all, there is a reason they are in care, right? If they had been more responsible and loving and less selfish, you wouldn't be the foster parent, right? But as we know, life is much more complicated than just one decision that led to a child coming into care. There are many factors that played a role. Perhaps it was mental illness, abuse, or poverty that led to desperation and addiction. Perhaps it was a generational and cyclical story that a family could not figure out how to reverse.

No matter what the story is, the biological parents of our children are people, too. They are oftentimes living in a world of hurt and distress. They have been faced with unimaginable suffering and loss, and while we so badly want to point fingers and play the blame game, we must remind ourselves that they are image bearers of God, and they deserve more than our pity and scoffing. They need our prayers, too.

The emotional rollercoaster of foster care is not for the faint of heart. There can be so much change and upheaval that one can feel jerked around within a matter of hours, as what you thought you knew turns out to be completely different. The biological parents of our children are in the midst of great grief, whether they acknowledge it or not. We cannot allow ourselves to sit in pride and think of all the ways that we are better than them. Our role as Christ followers is to point them to Jesus as well. It is not our role to take care of their children so that we get to keep them and live happily ever after. Because the goal of foster care is always reunification, we must live as though we believe that the biological parents of our children are worth investing in, too. We must come alongside and learn from them, recognizing that they may have something to offer to us that can help their child, too.

It seems counterintuitive to pray for someone that we may see as the enemy. We may deal with feelings of anger and a deep sense of betrayal when we think about our child's biological parents, especially if they were the perpetrator of the abuse that led to their foster care situation. However, if there is a possibility for reunification, we have to fight for the parent as well as the child. God created families to be together. His best design is for families to live and grow in unity as they learn to sacrificially love one another. We cannot fix anyone, but we can point them to Christ and advocate for restoration.

One of the greatest temptations we may have is to speak ill of our children's biological parents. But we must speak of them with honor and clarify the difference between being frustrated with their sin and not loving them as a person. Because the truth is that we are all just one bad decision away from a lifetime of hurt and regret, too.

We cannot allow our pride to get in the way of honoring the Lord with our speech as we seek to give our children's parents dignity and respect.

**Prayer**

Father, I have such mixed feelings toward the biological parents of my child. I so badly wish I got to be the one to raise them from the very beginning so that I could have sheltered them from all of the pain and heartache they have endured. When I think about all that my child has been through, it hurts my heart. But I also know that nothing is wasted in Your kingdom. You use every single thing in our lives, even the parts that feel insignificant, and You make them matter. I admit that I do not understand the world that the biological parents of my child are living in—it is completely different than mine. I want so badly for them to know You and to find peace and joy. Your word says that nothing is impossible with You, so I am praying for what seems impossible. I ask that You move in their hearts and show them Your love for them. Help them to know that You want to know them and be known by them. Help them to find the truth and be set free. Help me know how to love them, whether that is up close or from afar. Father, draw them to Your heart.

**Scripture to Declare**

And have mercy on those who doubt; save others by snatching them out of the fire; to others show mercy with fear, hating even the garment stained by the flesh. - Jude 22-23

# Day 18: Judges

*You shall do no injustice in court. You shall not be partial to the poor or defer to the great, but in righteousness shall you judge your neighbor.* - Leviticus 19:15

When we became foster parents, I remember being so nervous about going to court. I had never been in a courtroom before, and I had no idea what to expect. My frame of reference for courtrooms was limited to movies and Judge Judy reruns that play in car service waiting rooms. Would people yell and shout and use all kinds of legal jargon I didn't understand? As it turns out, court was not a big to-do and was much more normal than I would have thought. The people in court are just that, ordinary people. And while there is a great deal of legal jargon I don't understand, there is also a lot of normal back and forth conversation about everyday things.

A judge "presides over the courtroom and decides whether abuse or neglect has occurred and whether the child needs to be removed from the home. The judge may rule that certain conditions must be met for the child to remain at home."[7] The role of the judge is critical within the lives of our children. The judge hears all of the evidence presented before him and makes decisions that will change the trajectory of our children's lives. Thus, our hope is that we have a fair judge who truly cares about the welfare of children. There are so many people involved in the lives of our children, and each has an important role.

In the Bible, God appointed judges to rule the Israelites because they needed righteous leaders. While we do not know the spiritual condition of the judges who rule over the family and juvenile courts that we visit with our children, we can pray for the truth to be revealed and for them to act in the interest of our children. Romans 13:4-5 says, "For the one in authority is God's servant for your good. But if you do wrong, be afraid, for rulers do not bear the sword for no reason. They are God's servants, agents of wrath to bring punishment on the wrongdoer. Therefore, it is necessary to submit to the authorities, not only because of possible punishment but also as a matter of conscience."

We can rest assured knowing that the judges in the courtrooms have been appointed by God, whether they recognize that or not. We can also know that God is the ultimate judge, and He will execute justice on behalf of our children. It is tempting to live in fear when we consider the power that a judge holds, but we can rest in the sovereignty of our good Father, who always acts in perfect justice and righteousness.

---

[7] Understanding Child Welfare and the Courts. (2016, October). Retrieved 2020, from https://www.childwelfare.gov/pubPDFs/cwandcourts.pdf

**Prayer**

Father, oftentimes I am so afraid to step into the courtroom. Every time I do, I know that there is so much riding on a matter of minutes in which the truth may or may not be presented. I know that the courtroom is not beyond Your reach. I also know that even though the judge holds a lot of power, he is not in Your place. You are the ultimate lawgiver and authority. You are the One Who ensures that righteousness is upheld and justice prevails. Lord, would You give supernatural insight and wisdom to the judge who preside over my children's case? I want them to receive the best care possible and have confidence in knowing that they will be taken care of even if or when they leave my home. Please give the judge the ability to see all sides of the situation and act in the best interest of my child.

**Scripture to Declare**

The king's heart is a stream of water in the hand of the Lord; he turns it wherever he will. Every way of a man is right in his own eyes, but the Lord weighs the heart. To do righteousness and justice is more acceptable to the Lord than sacrifice. - Proverbs 21:1-3

The heavens declare his righteousness, for God himself is judge! - Psalm 50:6

For to us a child is born, to us a son is given; and the government shall be upon his shoulder, and his name shall be called Wonderful Counselor, Mighty God, Everlasting Father, Prince of Peace. - Isaiah 9:6

# Day 19: Attorneys

*May he defend the cause of the poor of the people, give deliverance to the children of the needy, and crush the oppressor! -Psalm 72:4*

As someone who was admittedly unfamiliar with the child welfare system and the courts, I remember being very overwhelmed by the sheer number of individuals involved in a child's case. The whole situation seemed cumbersome and difficult to navigate. The matter of foster care is not a simple one, and each case involves many different people. An attorney is appointed for each individual involved in a case. One case may have as many as four attorneys, as there is someone who represents the biological parent(s), the agency, the child, and in some cases, the foster parent. With so many voices in the midst of an already complicated situation, sometimes it is hard for the truth to prevail.

I remember being so frustrated when it seemed as though the truth was not being represented or considered in the midst of a case. It seemed as though the biological parents were the ones who were being heard and that some of the professionals involved were taking their side. The mama bear in me dealt with a good amount of righteous anger as I considered the welfare of my child and begged God to intervene. It was excruciatingly difficult to sit and hear how the truth was not being revealed.

We are blessed to have a care team who not only provides meals and helps with practical things like transportation and childcare, but also prays. This is their main way of serving us, and we could not be more grateful. Their prayers have changed things for eternity! There was one court date that was especially pivotal, and we specifically asked for our team to pray that the truth would be revealed. Well, this court date was like no other. I was given the opportunity to speak! The county workers and attorneys all listened to what I had to say, and considered it as they presented their thoughts to the judge. I had the privilege of advocating for my child!

An attorney is someone who investigates the facts of the case and in turn represents an individual who played a role in the situation at hand. Sometimes an attorney may represent a guilty party. Can you imagine the ethical turmoil that the attorney must feel as they are trying to advocate for someone who has played a role in bringing hurt and devastation to the life of a child? There is no easy way to do that. In fact, it may anger and upset us that a guilty person is allowed to have an advocate on their side. Why should they get a chance when they ruined the life of the precious child in our care?

When we are tempted to question the child welfare system and its intentions, we must go back to the truth of the Gospel. The truth is that while we were still sinners, Christ died for us (Romans 5) We have an intercessor Who constantly whispers our name to the Father and advocates for us, in spite of what we have done and will do to dishonor His name. So let us remember that while we cannot control the court system, we can give thanks for the sovereignty of our Heavenly Father, whose Son acts as the perfect attorney.

**Prayer**

Father, I cannot imagine the pressure that the attorneys are under. It is so much work to understand the details of a case and to represent their client with fairness. I know that the attorneys' job is not to please everyone, and to do so would be impossible. I know that You have given each attorney a client that plays a different role in this case. It is hard for me to understand how all of this tangled mess will ever get sorted out, and I struggle to believe that You can bring glory out of this. But I know that You work through imperfect people to enact Your judgements and Your plan. Please allow the attorneys involved in this case to uncover the truth. Your word says that when we know the truth, it will set us free. I pray that Your truth would be revealed and that lives would be changed as a result. Please give each attorney wisdom, insight, and a heart of honesty as they prepare for each court date. I ask for clear communication and Kingdom results, in Jesus' name.

**Scripture to Declare**

No one after lighting a lamp covers it with a jar or puts it under a bed, but puts it on a stand, so that those who enter may see the light. For nothing is hidden that will not be made manifest, nor is anything secret that will not be known and come to light. Take care then how you hear, for to the one who has, more will be given, and from the one who has not, even what he thinks that he has will be taken away. - Luke 8:16-18

By this we know love, that he laid down his life for us, and we ought to lay down our lives for the brothers. But if anyone has the world's goods and sees his brother in need, yet closes his heart against him, how does God's love abide in him? Little children, let us not love in word or talk but in deed and in truth. - 1 John 3:16-18

He will render to each one according to his works: to those who by patience in well-doing seek for glory and honor and immortality, he will give eternal life; but for those who are self-seeking and do not obey the truth, but obey unrighteousness, there will be wrath and fury. For God shows no partiality. - Romans 2:6-8, 11

# Day 20: Counselors

*Where there is no guidance, a people falls, but in an abundance of counselors there is safety. - Proverbs 11:14*

As a child, I wrote in journals. I would talk about my day and about the cute boy in math class. But as I grew and matured, my journals became a place for me to process all that was going on inside of me, and there was a lot going on. My journals were a place where I could put on paper the jumbled mess that was inside my heart and mind. During childhood, I experienced an incident with sexual abuse that I did not disclose until years after it happened. This made my mind a very confusing place to be at times. At the beginning of my husband and my relationship, this unresolved trauma exposed itself and came to an ugly head. Everything I had been stuffing for so many years finally said, "Enough!" and came out of the darkness so that the light of God's love could pour out His healing over my heart and soul.

Children in care have been through hard things. Sadly, we will never know their full stories. How could we? We do, however, have the privilege of knowing them in the present. And in the present, they are in our care in order to experience healing and growth. For years, people within the Christian community have not understood the value of counseling. It has sometimes been seen as unnecessary or as a crutch, because all we need is Jesus, right? And to that I say, yes, all we need is Jesus. But Jesus provides for us in myriad ways. He works through the members of the body of Christ to bring us healing.

I remember the first day I stepped into a counselor's office. At 26 years old, I was terrified to tell my story and to be honest with someone about things I had kept hidden for so long. Shame covered me like a cloak, and there was so much fear of the unknown. My husband and then fiancé offered to go with me so that I didn't have to be alone. But when I stepped into the office, I remember that the peace of Christ washed over me as I began to unload burdens I had been carrying for far too long.

Our children from hard places need the reassurance that they are not alone. They need trained professionals who can help them walk through overwhelming feelings and complicated life circumstances. Talking with a third party individual is incredibly helpful for processing your story. Finding a good counselor is not easy, and the first person may not be the best fit. That is ok. This part of our child's life is so important that we have to take the time to find the fit that is right for them. There is something to be said for our mental and emotional health as well. Secondary trauma can occur when we are caring for children from hard places. The more we process our story and enter into our healing, the better equipped we are to walk alongside our children. We can benefit from counseling, too, whether it is from a licensed professional or an older and wiser mentor. God speaks through various people in our lives to help us receive His truth.

**Prayer**

Father, I believe in the importance of a good counselor. I know that counseling is helpful as my child walks through their story. There are many broken pieces in their story, but You can help them put them together with the help of a counselor. Thank You for counselors and their role in listening to and walking alongside children. I ask that You provide the right counselor for my child so that they can feel comfortable expressing their needs and processing their hurts. Lord, I also ask that You provide a good counselor for me. I want to be able to serve from a place of abundance and peace. I know that I cannot do that if I continue to hold on to hurts and refuse to process difficulties in my story. I ask that You help me process what I am going through so that I can help my child do the same.

**Scripture to Declare**

Your testimonies are my delight; they are my counselors. - Psalm 119:24

For to us a child is born, to us a son is given; and the government shall be upon his shoulder, and his name shall be called Wonderful Counselor, Mighty God, Everlasting Father, Prince of Peace. - Isaiah 9:6

# Day 21: Social Workers

*Whatever you do, work heartily, as for the Lord and not for men, knowing that from the Lord you will receive the inheritance as your reward. You are serving the Lord Christ. - Colossians 3:23-24*

Chances are that if you have been working within the foster care system for long, you know the reputation that county social workers have amongst foster parents. In fact, many people are afraid to become foster parents because they have heard horror stories about what it was like to work with the county. During our first foster care experience, we had one of those horror stories. We found ourselves in the midst of a difficult situation at home that was made even more difficult by the lack of support we had. It was overwhelming, frustrating, and maddening. We looked at each other and said, "Now I can understand why some people do this once and never do it again." Things were just so hard.

After taking a break and saying yes to a new placement, we have had a completely different experience and received so much support. We have enjoyed fellowship with county workers who are believers and who understand the calling we have said yes too as one from God. Things are completely different than our first go-round, and we could have missed so much if we had said no simply out of fear and bitterness.

County social workers are often overworked and underpaid. They have the insurmountable job of overseeing the welfare of ridiculous numbers of children. They carry the heartbreaking stories of these children and their families with them as they also try to navigate what it looks like to be parents themselves. Can you imagine the pressure and the fear that would come with this role? To know that you can only do so much to ensure the welfare of a child when the judge could make a decision that is completely the opposite of what you believe to be beneficial for this child? Can you imagine the heartache that occurs when a teenager runs away again and is missing and you just want to go home and hang out with your family?

There are many social workers who truly care about the children they serve, and there are some who are jaded and burnt out. We cannot allow their bitterness or unresolved issues to stop us from loving the children to whom God has called us. The social workers play a vital role in allowing us to be matched with children who will suit our family's needs and abilities, and they also are a vital part of child's life, no matter how many placements they may have endured.

We have all experienced a time when we could not get in touch with a social worker and felt frustrated at their lack of response. What if the next time that happens, instead of complaining, we recognize God's sovereignty over the situation? What if we respond to them in kindness when they do get in touch instead of acting exasperated and annoyed? What if we asked them if we could pray for them and how we could support them as they support our children and our families?

You may know a social worker who is kind, supportive, and patient. You may know a social worker who is jaded, burnt out, and over it. Either way, this person is an image bearer who deserves your kindness and respect. Let's make the choice to love them, too.

**Prayer**

Father, thank You for the social workers in my life. Thank You for my resource director who cares for our family and ensures that we are in a good place and able to care for our kids. Thank You for my child's social worker, who ensures that he is taken care of and that he gets everything he needs. I pray that You would help me to be a source of encouragement to all of the county workers that I interact with. It is tempting to be demanding and to rationalize rude behavior when I am tired and frustrated with this whole system. But I know that the brokenness of this system is why you call believers like me to be a part of it. You want us to know that Your light shines brightest in the darkest places. Lord, help me to know how to be kind and courteous at all times, but also to be firm and fight for my children and my family. You are enough for me, and I want others to know Your love as a result of coming into contact with our family.

**Scripture to Declare**

Behold, I am sending you out as sheep in the midst of wolves, so be wise as serpents and innocent as doves. Beware of men, for they will deliver you over to courts and flog you in their synagogues, and you will be dragged before governors and kings for my sake, to bear witness before them and the Gentiles. When they deliver you over, do not be anxious how you are to speak or what you are to say, for what you are to say will be given to you in that hour. For it is not you who speak, but the Spirit of your Father speaking through you. - Matthew 10:16-20

# Day 22: CASA Volunteers

*Learn to do good; seek justice, correct oppression; bring justice to the fatherless, plead the widow's cause. - Isaiah 1:17*

A CASA is a Court Appointed Special Advocate, and in some cases, this person may serve as a guardian ad litem for your child. This person is a hero in your foster care tribe. Every foster parent longs for one because we understand the power that they hold. A CASA is someone who takes the time to be trained and understand the ins and outs of the foster care system. During that time, they learn about how to advocate for children by understanding every aspect of the situation. Not only do they take the time to get to know the child in care, but they also learn about and interview the parents and other family members. They learn absolutely everything they can about the case so that they can stand before the judge with an informed opinion about what would be best for the child. They get to know the foster parents and learn about them so that they can understand whether the child is growing and thriving in the home. Theirs is an important position.

Unlike social workers and counselors who are paid by the state to be a part of your child's life, this person takes the time on a completely voluntary basis to get involved and advocate for the truth to be revealed and for justice to prevail. Each time there is a court hearing, the CASA writes a report on the latest happenings so that the judge is informed and understands what is going on in the lives of all who are involved in the case. This person's role cannot be underestimated.

I have found that a CASA is someone who cares about children and wants to make a difference in the community by serving families. They believe in investing in the lives of vulnerable children and want to do whatever they can to help them. One of the things I love about having a CASA for my kids is that it gives our family an opportunity to share the light of Christ with yet another person who may need Him. Because the CASA has to know everything there is to know about the child's case, your family is once again given the opportunity to let someone else in and show them how you do life. What a beautiful way to display the Gospel and hope of Jesus Christ. If your child does not have a CASA, pray for one and share with others this way to get involved in the foster care system.

**Prayer**

Father, I thank You for the valuable work of CASA volunteers. It is incredible to me the village that it takes to raise a child, let alone a child in care. I know that the people whom You have entrusted with my child's story are people who care and who long to see hope realized and lives changed. My prayer is that these volunteers would be able to uncover the truth and present it with accuracy and compassion so that the judge is able to act on behalf of the child. Thank You that the CASA is able to understand everything that is going on with my child's case, even when I can't. Thank You for the tireless work that they take on in order to uncover all of the facts. I ask that You allow our lives to speak to them and to show them the beauty of a life lived surrendered to You. Help them to see our lives and understand the power of the Gospel, and give us opportunities to share the Gospel with them.

**Scripture to Declare**

Greater love has no one than this, that someone lay down his life for his friends. - John 15:13

The Lord is my light and my salvation; whom shall I fear? The Lord is the stronghold of my life; of whom shall I be afraid? - Psalm 27:1

# Day 23: Healthcare Providers

*Bless the Lord, O my soul, and forget not all his benefits, who forgives all your iniquity, who heals all your diseases, who redeems your life from the pit, who crowns you with steadfast love and mercy, who satisfies you with good so that your youth is renewed like the eagle's. -Psalm 103:2-5*

When a child comes into your home, there are so many needs—mental, emotional, spiritual, and physical. Many of us became foster parents because we wanted to be a part of helping to bring healing to the mental, emotional, and spiritual aspects of children's lives. However, when we look at the works of Jesus in the New Testament, we see that He often brought healing to the spiritual and the physical simultaneously. The Pharisees—a religious and legalistic group of that time period—were often dumbfounded by Jesus' boldness to forgive sins, claiming blasphemy.

Children from hard places have physical needs that require physical healing. Some may be malnourished. Others may not have received dental care. Still others may not have received proper hygiene care and as a result have infections. The list goes on and on.

Our children need to be able to feel at home in their bodies and know that their bodies were made for good by a Creator who loves them. They need to know that they are fearfully and wonderfully made, and that when in Christ, their body is a temple of the Holy Spirit who dwells within.

Healthcare providers operate by the mantra "Do no harm." They want children to thrive and not just survive. As their parents, our desire is the same. We want our children to be taken care of and receive the dignity they deserve, simply because they are children. They cannot take care of themselves, and we want to be a part of ensuring that they know they are worthy of care and attention. Healthcare providers play an important role in the lives of our children, as they provide guidance and make decisions about medication, diet, and lifestyle habits.

As we deal with county guidelines and all kinds of bureaucracy regarding how we can obtain the medication and resources that our children sometimes need to thrive, we can get frustrated. But let us remember that God knows all of our children's needs. He understands exactly what will bring healing to our children's hearts *and* bodies. And we can trust that as we collaborate with providers and professionals, He will lead us to the right people for our children and meet their needs.

**Prayer**

Father, sometimes I am overwhelmed by the sheer amount of need that is presented before me in the life of my child. I know that their needs are great, and I want to figure out how those needs can be met. I know that healthcare providers are only vessels that You work through, and they won't always have all of the answers. The only thing that I can do is surrender my child over to You again and again. I want to trust that even if there is physical healing that needs to take place that seems insurmountable, that You are the God of the impossible. I want to believe that nothing is too difficult for You. So Father, I pray for the healthcare providers who will care for my children. Please give them the Spirit of wisdom and revelation to see the root causes of any health issues present within my child's body. Help them to look at their whole history and to holistically serve them so that they thrive and are able to walk in health and healing.

**Scripture to Declare**

Heal me, O Lord, and I shall be healed; save me, and I shall be saved, for you are my praise. - Jeremiah 17:14

Beloved, I pray that all may go well with you and that you may be in good health, as it goes well with your soul. - 3 John 1:2

# Day 24: Fellow Foster Parents

*A cord of three strands is not quickly broken. - Ephesians 4:12*

I remember the summer that we had our first placement, and I felt like I was going crazy in some moments. It was so much harder than I had imagined it would be, and there were days when I felt like I was drowning. Thankfully, there are many other foster parents within our community, and there was a little group text thread of fellow foster mamas in which I was able to pour out my heart and my frustrations. These women became a lifeline to me because they truly understood what I was going through. Even though no two cases are alike, there were many shared experiences, feelings, and frustrations with which they could empathize.

Each year, my husband and I attend a conference that provides more than half of our required annual training hours. One year, a sweet couple mentioned that they were the only couple at their church who was fostering and that they did not know any other foster parents. And yet they had two placements in their home and were open to more children in care. I was amazed at their strength and resolve to continue to care for vulnerable children even without a community of people who were walking the same path. What an incredible witness to their faithfulness.

We were made for community, and we were made to encourage one another. I simply cannot imagine what our fostering journey would look like if I didn't have friends who were on the same path and who paved the way for me and inspired me to say yes. If you don't have those people in your actual real life, pray for God to bring them to you!

As a foster parent, it is easy for us to completely be consumed by all that is going on in our home. But there is also so much power when we realize that others are walking this road, and we can partner with them in prayer. We often say, "The only thing I have left is prayer," but prayer is the most important work we can do and the best gift that we can give to others. We have personally seen so much breakthrough when we have partnered with other foster parents in prayer and when they have come alongside us as well. Today, let's remember our fellow foster parents in prayer.

**Prayer**

Father, thank You for the unique call of fostering. Thank You that there are other people who have nontraditional families. Thank You that You have called us to do hard and different things but have not left us to do it all alone. I pray for my fellow foster parent friends. Thank You for their boldness and willingness to enter into brokenness. Thank You for the sacrifices they have made. I ask that You fill them with the knowledge of Your goodness and with the peace that passes all understanding. Fix their eyes on You and root them deeply in Your love. Give them all the strength they need to not give up and to fight for their children—biological, foster, and adopted. Help them to prioritize their marriage and give their spouse the benefit of the doubt in the midst of miscommunications and misunderstandings. Give them joy that sustains and overwhelms them. Help them shine their light brightly so that others can see the beauty of this calling.

**Scripture to Declare**

Two are better than one, because they have a good return for their labor: If either of them falls down, one can help the other up. But pity anyone who falls and has no one to help them up. Also, if two lie down together, they will keep warm. But how can one keep warm alone? Though one may be overpowered, two can defend themselves. A cord of three strands is not quickly broken. - Ecclesiastes 4:9-12

Blessed be the God and Father of our Lord Jesus Christ, the Father of mercies and God of all comfort, who comforts us in all our affliction, so that we may be able to comfort those who are in any affliction, with the comfort with which we ourselves are comforted by God. For as we share abundantly in Christ's sufferings, so through Christ we share abundantly in comfort too. - 2 Corinthians 1:3-5

# Day 25: Church Family

*A new commandment I give to you, that you love one another: just as I have loved you, you also are to love one another. By this all people will know that you are my disciples, if you have love for one another. - John 13:34-35*

Many people say that the call to care for widows and orphans is a command given in Scripture. However, when one looks closely at the language of the oft quoted verse in James, there is no imperative language. James 1:27 states, "Religion that is pure and undefiled before God the Father is this: to visit orphans and widows in their affliction, and to keep oneself unstained from the world." In Greek, "to visit" means "to look upon in order to help or benefit." The work of foster care is summed up quite well in this definition. However, there are other verses in Scripture that encourage the family of God to care for the vulnerable.

Isaiah 1:17 says, "Learn to do good; seek justice, correct oppression; bring justice to the fatherless, plead the widow's cause." And Deuteronomy 10:18 says, "He executes justice for the fatherless and the widow, and loves the sojourner, giving him food and clothing." Foster families seek to not only provide for the physical needs of vulnerable children, but also to bring justice to their lives by advocating for their best interests. We know that as foster parents, there is a community of people upholding the foster family so that they can continue to serve and pour out on the children whom the Lord has entrusted to them. The church family should make up a big part of that community.

You have probably had some or all of the following said to you from well-meaning individuals:

"I don't know how you do it."

"You're incredible."

"You sure have your hands full!"

Our goal when fostering is to shine a light in the darkest places in a child's life. When we choose to say yes to this calling, we also say yes to shining a light within our church family in order to help them see the beauty of obedience in the hard places. Jesus encouraged the disciples to "let your light shine before others, so that they may see your good works and give glory to your Father who is in heaven." The call to fostering is a difficult one, full of many surprises and emotional rollercoasters, sometimes within just one day! To walk this road is to walk a road of deep trust and sacrifice.

One of the biggest comforts to us when we began fostering was the ability to be up close and personal in the lives of others who had gone before us. When we saw ordinary people just like us say yes to foster care, we realized that it didn't take a "special person" or a "super Christian" to do it. It just took a willing and available heart. Perhaps your family is an example for another within your church who is considering the call but unsure of whether they are ready to say yes. Hebrews 10:24 encourages the family of God to "consider how to stir up one another to love and good works." Your family may be the one to help others say yes to this hard but worthy calling.

**Prayer**

Father, thank You for my church family. Thank You for the way they love You and for the way they encourage me to love You more. I ask that You help me to speak truth with kindness and to be an example to them. Father, I also ask that You keep me humble. People often compliment me and tell me how wonderful I am for being a foster parent. This sometimes makes me uncomfortable, but it also puffs me up a bit and strokes my ego. I do not want to act as though I am any better than anyone else. I know how often I fail and fall, but I am so grateful for Your grace and mercy. Father, I pray that You use my imperfect willingness and obedience to spur someone else to say yes to this calling. Help others to see the rich and beautiful goodness that is found when they are a part of a child's life.

**Scripture to Declare**

But now in Christ Jesus you who once were far off have been brought near by the blood of Christ. For he himself is our peace, who has made us both one and has broken down in his flesh the dividing wall of hostility by abolishing the law of commandments expressed in ordinances, that he might create in himself one new man in place of the two, so making peace, and might reconcile us both to God in one body through the cross, thereby killing the hostility. And he came and preached peace to you who were far off and peace to those who were near. For through him we both have access in one Spirit to the Father. So then you are no longer strangers and aliens, but you are fellow citizens with the saints and members of the household of God, built on the foundation of the apostles and prophets, Christ Jesus himself being the cornerstone, in whom the whole structure, being joined together, grows into a holy temple in the Lord. In him you also are being built together into a dwelling place for God by the Spirit. - Ephesians   2:13-22

# Day 26: Outsiders Looking In

*And your ancient ruins shall be rebuilt; you shall raise up the foundations of many generations; you shall be called the repairer of the breach, the restorer of streets to dwell in.* - Isaiah 58:12

The kingdom of God is upside down and completely different from the world's standards of what is "the good life." The American dream itself consists of self-made goals and accomplishments. The hope of many is to find a way to work the least that they can and play as much as they can. But God's kingdom is the total opposite. He asks us to take up our cross and follow Him. He tells us to find joy and peace in laying down our lives and sacrificing our comforts for His ways.

Chances are, your family does not look like others in your area. You may have children of different races or a larger family with multiple children. You may get a lot of questions about your family from others who want to know about how your family came to be. When inquiring minds want to know - like neighbors, store clerks, and coworkers - you have an opportunity to share with them about the calling you have been given by God.

The truth is that our lives should look different than those around us. Our lives are supposed to be set apart for God's glory. When we do the work of fostering, we are destroying generational curses and taking back ground that the enemy has stolen for his reign. We are building the kingdom of God, and when we do this, people will take notice. Sometimes, we may be tempted to be annoyed when people ask insensitive questions or pry into our family's history. But during these moments, we can choose to use our story for His glory. We can choose to lift up the name of Jesus and give people insight into living a life surrendered to Him.

One of the most beautiful parts of foster care is getting a front row seat to redemption stories. Being part of these stories is a great privilege, and while we cannot share the intimate details of these stories with random passersby, we can give others a glimpse into the true good life—a life full of deep and hard-earned joy.

**Prayer**

Father, I know that people are very curious about our life as a foster family. I know that they want to know how in the world we came to all be together. This is a beautiful thing—the curiosity about how You built our family. When people want to know our story, help me know what parts to share. I pray that our story encourages their hearts and shows them the beauty of living life Your way—surrendered and free. May they be moved to find the joy of knowing You through whatever adventure You have written for them.

**Scripture to Declare**

For by grace you have been saved through faith. And this is not your own doing; it is the gift of God, not a result of works, so that no one may boast. For we are his workmanship, created in Christ Jesus for good works, which God prepared beforehand, that we should walk in them - Ephesians 2:8-10

In the same way, let your light shine before others, so that they may see your good works and give glory to your Father who is in heaven. - Matthew 5:16

# Day 27: Spiritual Health

*He is like a tree planted by streams of water that yields its fruit in its season, and its leaf does not wither. In all that he does, he prospers.* - Psalm 1:2

Our spiritual health is the most important part of who we are, and yet it is often the first thing we neglect when we are in survival mode. Oftentimes, foster parenting can be characterized by one season of survival mode after another. But the Word is full of exhortations to abide, rest, and thrive in the presence of the Lord. This thriving in His presence is not found through just surviving from one day to the next. His deep and abiding joy is found in a well that has been dug deep to taste of His riches and be sustained by them in order to pour out on others in need of His abundant grace and mercy. I have a tendency to want to do everything on my own. But the fact is that I was made to need my Savior. I was not created for an autonomous life.

There are times when I get so wrapped up in my to-do list and all that has to be done that I neglect to sit at the feet of my

Savior. I don't forget to do it, because I know the importance of coming to Him. But I hope that just a few minutes will "get me through." The beautiful thing about Christianity is that it is a relationship, not a religion. When you are in a relationship, you take time to get to know someone. No one had to force me to spend time with my husband when we were dating. Every moment that I could spend with him was precious and not taken for granted. Each conversation was exciting and new.

If we have been walking with God and grow tired and weary, chances are that we have lost the art of sitting at His feet. His Word tells us that His mercies are new every morning and that His love never runs dry. His grace is sufficient for us, because His power is made perfect in our weaknesses. He is always doing a new thing, and He wants to bring good out of each situation in our lives and thereby bring glory to His name. Our entire mission as foster parents is not to save our children. We cannot do that. Our mission is to love them with the love of Christ and give them a safe place to land, for however long that may be. We cannot give what we do not have. If we do not have a relationship with Christ that is built on the truth of His word, we won't be able to give that to our children. Thus, our spiritual health has to be tantamount to everything else.

We may not be able to get up in the morning and spend hours reading the Word. We may not have hundreds of verses memorized. But I am encouraged by my pastor and friend Carlos Sibley, who has stated to meditate on the Word is to allow it to get inside of you and read *you*, changing you from the inside out. To be in an abiding relationship with the Lord is to continually direct our gaze toward Him, adoring Him and drawing upon His perfect strength when we fail. This is the Gospel - to be made new over and over again because we are in desperate need of a Savior.

**Prayer**

Father, I admit that sometimes I do not take care of my spiritual health. I neglect to spend time with You because I think that it can wait and that I don't have time to really "make it count." But I know that Your word and Your presence are what will sustain and satisfy me. Help me to feast on Your word and not be spiritually apathetic. Help me to love Your word more than I love anything else, for Your word gives life. I need You, Father. Help me to love You with all that I am.

**Scripture to Declare**

But he answered, "It is written, 'Man shall not live by bread alone, but by every word that comes from the mouth of God.'" Matthew 4:4

My soul clings to the dust; give me life according to your word! Make me understand the way of your precepts, and I will meditate on your wondrous works. - Psalm 119:25, 27

# Day 28: Surrender

*Humble yourselves, therefore, under the mighty hand of God so that at the proper time he may exalt you, casting all your anxieties on him, because he cares for you.* - 1 Peter 5:6-7

Hi, my name is Jessica, and I am a control freak. Call it a character flaw or a quirk of my personality, but I really like to have a plan. I thrive on routine and a sense of predictability. But foster care is anything but routine and predictable. We welcome children into our homes with very limited information, learning about them as the days go on. We say yes to their trauma, family history, and ways of life. We blindly agree to love and care for them.

When a child enters our home, we often have an idea of how things would go if we were in charge. We assess the situation and think to ourselves, "If this happens, then this happens, then this child will be taken care of and come out of this thing relatively unscathed." But we fool ourselves into thinking that we know what is best when in fact we have quite a limited understanding of all that is going on in the lives of everyone involved. Foster care is full of heartache and disappointment, and if we are not living from a place of surrender, we can find ourselves being tossed and turned about by the constant change.

Imagine being ripped away from everything you knew and being placed in a home with strangers who were happy to see you and so excited that you were there. Regardless of your history and the trauma you endured, everything is still overwhelming and strange. You have now had to surrender everything to the state, of which you are now a ward. You may only have the clothes on your back, and nothing is familiar. Your surroundings are new, and you may not even be with your siblings, who are a source of comfort for you. But the grown ups keep telling you that everything is going to be ok and that they are there to help you. Can you imagine just for a moment what it would be like to be a child in care? How it would feel to go through so much change in such a short amount of time?

As the adults in this situation, we have the ability to process things through the lens of experience, wisdom, and maturity. And yet we still find ourselves at a loss for what to say or do when circumstances prove to be so very difficult. This is why we must live surrendered lives to Jesus. We must advocate for our children and fight for their best interests while still holding our plans loosely. We know that God is sovereign and good. And because He is sovereign and good, He will work all things out for His glory—it just may not be the way we want it to be. Psalm 91:1-2 says, "He who dwells in the shelter of the Most High will abide in the shadow of the Almighty. I will say to the Lord, 'My refuge and my fortress, my God, in whom I trust.'" When we make the Lord our dwelling place and trust Him in all things, we can know that He is with us, for us, and not against us - and the same can be said for our precious children and their lives.

**Prayer**

Father, there are so many parts of foster care that are difficult to process. I do not understand everything that is going on and know that I most likely never will. There are so many people involved and so many decisions made of which I am completely unaware. I want so badly to just tell everyone what to do and ensure that people make the right choices. But I know that is impossible. However, I know that I am not powerless. Your Word tells the story of the power of prayer. You have shown me the importance of bringing everything before Your throne and leaving it there. So Father, help me to see prayer as my first defense and not as a last resort. Help me to trust You with everything. I surrender my comfort and my thoughts about what is best to You. I say with faith and conviction that You are good, and You make all things new. I trust You.

**Scripture to Declare**

And we know that for those who love God all things work together for good, for those who are called according to his purpose. - Romans 8:28

You keep him in perfect peace whose mind is stayed on you, because he trusts in you. - Isaiah 26:3

# Day 29: The Future

*I will say to the Lord, "My refuge and my fortress, my God, in whom I trust."- Psalm 91:2*

Corrie ten Boom said, "Never be afraid to trust an unknown future to a known God." When we have welcomed children from hard places into our home, we can easily be afraid of the future. I remember the anxiety and fear that plagued me almost constantly during our first placement. We were in way over our heads and dealing with behaviors that were extremely difficult to navigate. The fear of the future robbed me of my peace and joy. I felt as though I were drowning under the weight of years of trauma by experiencing secondary trauma. The only thing I could do was look at the moment right in front of me, for to look to the next day was crushing.

The absolute worst thing we can do as parents is to parent from a place of fear. Fear paralyzes and steals. Fear distorts and discourages. Faith mobilizes and gives. Faith empowers and emboldens. It is tempting as a parent to look at daily struggles and only see the long view. We believe if a child is struggling with lying right now, he or she is forever doomed to be a pathological liar who never tells the truth. Within the foster care realm, we may look at the circumstances of a child's case and think that there is no hope for the adults involved to get to a place where they can care for their child. But we serve a God who loves to rewrite the future, regardless of the past.

Isaiah 43:18-19 says, "Remember not the former things, nor consider the things of old. Behold, I am doing a new thing; now it springs forth, do you not perceive it?" Oftentimes, we are afraid of the future because we are dwelling on the past. We look at all that has happened in the past and see the transgressions and heartache and cannot fathom what the future holds if the past is so broken. But God is all about writing a new story. He is about redemption, restoration, and renewed hope.

When we look at the future and are afraid, we can look back at the faithfulness of God in the past and know that He is good and will continue to be. God cannot change and cannot lie. All that He does is kind and gracious. Thus, we can trust Him and know that the future we fear is already in His hands.

**Prayer**

Father, I look at the future and I don't see a way around all of the destruction and difficulty. But You are the God who makes a way where there is no way. You are the only One who can make dead bones live and cause hope to arise in the midst of hopeless situations. Help me to trust that You truly are enough for all of my worries and fears. Thank You for never leaving or forsaking me. Help me to walk by faith and not by sight. Show me how to rest in Your goodness by knowing that the future is held in Your hands and that You will carry me. Help me show my children that You are a God of great intention and care, and You will shelter us in Your perfect love.

**Scripture to Declare**

And without faith it is impossible to please him, for whoever would draw near to God must believe that he exists and that he rewards those who seek him. - Hebrews 11:6

Now faith is the assurance of things hoped for, the conviction of things not seen. - Hebrews 11:1

# Day 30: Fear vs. Faith

*For God gave us a spirit not of fear but of power and love and self-control. - 2 Timothy 1:7*

"*Lord, I need You.*"

"*I feel so afraid.*"

"*I feel so alone.*"

"*Help me.*"

"*I'm drowning and overwhelmed.*"

There are days, weeks, and months during this journey of fostering that fear can threaten us and lurk so readily, just waiting to be fed. When a child exhibits extreme behaviors. When a biological parent does not cooperate. When a case worker misunderstands your intentions. When a family member makes an offhand comment. Fear, if we allow it, can play a major role in our mental, emotional, and spiritual health. Fear is not a negative emotion. Emotions in and of themselves are neutral and do not have a moral value. However, *misplaced* fear is what can lead us astray.

All throughout the Bible, God speaks to us about fear. Some have said that there is some version of "Do not fear" 365 times in His word - one for every day of the year. But He also tells us that "the fear of the Lord is the beginning of wisdom" (Proverbs 1:7). Psychologists will tell you that fear is a healthy emotion, because fear can protect you from danger! But when fear is misplaced, it can paralyze you. Imagine if you had been too afraid to step into the journey of fostering. How different would your life look? What treasures would you not have discovered through this journey?

Fear can be a determining factor that hinders us when we do not surrender it to the Lord. During our first placement, I remember being so afraid due to one child's extreme and violent behaviors. The anxiety made me physically ill and haunted me through the days. There was a constant battle in my mind, and I had to pray and tell the Lord that I trusted Him, even when I didn't feel that trust.

Some of us are afraid that the county agency will not make decisions that are in the best interest of our children. We have seen children not valued and tossed to and fro because of adults' poor choices. This fear of whether or not they will be taken care of is rooted in our deep love for their well being and our desire for them to be treated with kindness and fairness.

On the opposite side of the spectrum, we have faith. When we cannot face another day and find ourselves exhausted by our limitations and overwhelmed by the lack of control, we can run to the Lord. When we are tempted to come undone because everything around us seems to be falling apart, we can look to the Lord and say, "Help me. I need You. Come be with me."

One of my favorite podcasts to listen to is *The Glorious in the Mundane* with singer and author Christy Nockels. In this podcast, she beautifully speaks about Scripture and its application to our everyday lives. She mentions the beauty of "breath prayers" - those short phrases that we mutter under our breath when we have little else to offer. So often we believe that we must spend hours in prayer in order to "make it count." But God can meet us in a moment and do more in one minute than we can try to do in a lifetime. His Holy Spirit is that powerful, sweet, and intentional.

Fear says, "What if _____ happens?" Faith says, "Even if _____ happens, my God is still good." When Shadrach, Meshach, and Abednego walked through the fiery furnace, their hope was in God to protect them. But they wisely stated that even if He didn't, He is still a good God. (Daniel 3:18) We are faced with extremely difficult situations through our fostering journeys. But we can know that even while our circumstances change (sometimes daily), we still serve a good God. He is with us, for us, and not against us. And resting in that can minimize our fears and magnify His presence.

**Prayer**

Father, sometimes I feel so afraid of all the things that could go wrong. I also feel afraid of myself - when things get really stressful and tense, I can feel myself begin to fall apart. I don't like how that feels. It is uncomfortable and frightening. To feel held together is so much more comfortable for me. But I know that You don't expect me to just "have it together" all the time. You are my source of peace. Help me to run to You when peace is hard to come by in our home and in my heart. I cannot do anything without You, Lord. I know that my children from hard places have operated in fear for most of their lives. They have been in survival mode because they did not have any other choice. But You have given them a fresh start by entrusting them to me, and I want to teach them how to walk in faith and know Your goodness. Help me to be an example of someone who trusts in You. Help me not to be shaken and consumed by fear, but rather to be wrapped up in faith, knowing that Your promises never fail.

**Scripture to Declare**

And Jesus answered them, "Truly, I say to you, if you have faith and do not doubt, you will not only do what has been done to the fig tree, but even if you say to this mountain, 'Be taken up and thrown into the sea,' it will happen." - Matthew 21:21

Therefore, since we are surrounded by so great a cloud of witnesses, let us also lay aside every weight, and sin which clings so closely, and let us run with endurance the race that is set before us, looking to Jesus, the founder and perfecter of our faith, who for the joy that was set before him endured the cross, despising the shame, and is seated at the right hand of the throne of God.- Hebrews 12:1-2

# Day 31: Thy Will

*I know you're good*

*But this don't feel good right now*

*And I know you think*

*Of things I could never think about*

*It's hard to count it all joy*

*Distracted by the noise*

*Just trying to make sense*

*Of all your promises*

*Sometimes I gotta stop*

*Remember that you're God*

*And I am not, so*

*Thy will be done*

*Thy will be done*

*Thy will be done*

*Like a child on my knees all that comes to me is*

*Thy will be done*

- Hilary Scott, "Thy Will"

 

The songwriter penned these lyrics after a miscarriage, which had sent her into a deep grief. Loss can send us to places we have never been before and create a desperation within us that is unfamiliar and uncomfortable. If there is one thing that properly sums up the journey of foster care, it is a story of loss. Our children have suffered loss after loss as they have had everything they know stripped away from them. They have not known a sense of normalcy and stability. We have endured loss when children come in and out of our homes without much time to prepare. All of the major players in foster care have known the death of a dream—whether that is a failed adoption or failed reunification. Loss permeates the story of foster care and threatens to choke the life out of us.

But God writes a different story and weaves together a tapestry of beauty within the brokenness. In the book of Ruth in the Bible, we see two women who are clinging to one another and clinging to God as they navigate loss. Naomi is Ruth's mother-in-law, and she has lost not only her husband but also her two sons. Ruth has lost her husband, and her sister-in-law has as well. The difference between Ruth and her sister-in Orpah is that Ruth decides to stay with Naomi and does not abandon her in her time of need. Naomi, however, is in the throes of her grief and asks for everyone to call her "Mara" because it means "bitter." (Naomi means "pleasant.") When these two women show up to Bethlehem, they are desperate for the kindness of others to help provide for them. God miraculously provides for them through the generosity of a man named Boaz, and Ruth ends up marrying this man of God and becoming a part of the family line of not only David, the righteous king, but also King Jesus.

Our children's stories are full of heartache and heaviness. When we enter into their stories, we have ideas about how God needs to change things so that they no longer experience these difficulties. We think we know exactly what needs to happen in order for our kids to be safe and cared for. Sometimes we are on the same page as God, and sometimes we are way off. His ways are higher than ours, and His thoughts are not our thoughts. (Isaiah 55:8) But one thing we can know for sure is that He is sovereign. This means that He is not asleep as people around us make choices (without consulting us! The audacity!). He is not unaware of our children's plight nor unwilling to move. He is with us, and He cares. He sees us. He knows us. He loves us. The same is true for our children.

While we can imagine the fairy tale ending, God has something in store that is so much better than anything that we could ever dream of. (Ephesians 3:20-21) When we surrender to His will, we say yes to Him. His word says that all the promises of God are yes and amen in Christ Jesus. (2 Corinthians 1:20) Let's trust Him to be who He says He is, and with confidence say with Jesus, "Not my will, but Yours be done."

**Prayer**

Father, I so badly want to control everything. I wish I knew the future and knew what was going to happen within this crazy world that is foster care. It is so hard to not be able to make decisions and to feel as though I am lost in the shuffle, when as the foster parent, I am on the front lines of my kids' lives every day. Help me not to be prideful and feel as though I deserve any recognition or power. I want to love You above all else, and that means that I surrender to Your will and trust You. Even when the circumstances look so dark and seem so overwhelming, I know that You are good. Even when there seems to be no way, I know that You will make a way. I trust You. Thy will be done.

**Scripture to Declare**

And he said, "Abba, Father, all things are possible for you. Remove this cup from me. Yet not what I will, but what you will."- Mark 14:36

Come to me, all who labor and are heavy laden, and I will give you rest. Take my yoke upon you, and learn from me, for I am gentle and lowly in heart, and you will find rest for your souls. For my yoke is easy, and my burden is light. - Matthew 11:28-30

# Day 32: Wisdom

*If any of you lacks wisdom, let him ask God, who gives generously to all without reproach, and it will be given him.* - James 1:5

Wisdom is "the soundness of an action or decision with regard to the application of experience, knowledge, and good judgment." Simply put, wisdom is being able to understand how to apply the knowledge one possesses. Without wisdom, we can make poor decisions and be guided by emotions, which are fickle. In a world where it is noble to "own your truth," and find comfort in "doing you," wisdom is much needed. Each day, the world says to "follow your heart." How do we know which way to turn?

Our world is overwhelming and confusing, but God is a God of peace, not confusion. (1 Corinthians 14:33) The work of foster care is messy and complicated. There are many opportunities for us to get it wrong. We can say the wrong thing or stay silent when we need to speak up. We can find ourselves drowning in all of the paperwork and records that we must keep. We can look to others to tell us how to parent when we know that we need God's voice to be the loudest.

In 1 Kings 3:16-28, we read of a story in which two mothers are arguing over a child. These women live in the same house together and give birth to babies within days of one another. But tragedy strikes one night when one of the mothers rolls over on her baby during her sleep, thereby killing him. In her distress, she swaps the baby for the other, hoping that the other mother will not notice. The matter of the baby's identity is brought before King Solomon for his wisdom and mediation. He states,

*"Divide the living child in two, and give half to the one and half to the other."*

*Then the woman whose son was alive said to the king, because her heart yearned for her son, "Oh, my lord, give her the living child, and by no means put him to death." But the other said, "He shall be neither mine nor yours; divide him." Then the king answered and said, "Give the living child to the first woman, and by no means put him to death; she is his mother." And all Israel heard of the judgment that the king had rendered, and they stood in awe of the king, because they perceived that the wisdom of God was in him to do justice. (1 Kings 3:25-28)*

We are hungry for justice to be served in our children's lives. But our hunger for justice must be measured by the wisdom of our God. Our emotions and desires are often at war within us. We want their biological parents to face consequences for their actions, but we also want them to receive mercy and find grace in the arms of a Savior who wants to redeem them. We want to teach our children the difference between right and wrong and help them navigate this world, but we also want to parent from a place of love and compassion. There are so many choices that we are presented with as foster parents every day. These choices can feel conflicting and confusing, but we serve a God of great wisdom who can help us navigate them with grace and truth. Let us run to Him and delight in His word so that we are prepared for whatever comes our way.

**Prayer**

Father, I need Your wisdom. I do not possess all that is necessary to parent well and to walk through this fostering journey. There are so many things I do not understand, and there are so many parts of this journey that are so heavy and hard. It is hard to learn and glean from other parents because our situation is so unique. Help me to come to You and rely on Your wisdom alone. I do not need the wisdom of others that can fail me. I need Your word. Show me truths in Your word that are specific to our situation that will help us. We cannot do anything without You, Lord. Give me eyes to see, ears to hear, and a heart to receive from You alone. You are good.

**Scripture to Declare**

For the Lord gives wisdom; from his mouth come knowledge and understanding; he stores up sound wisdom for the upright; he is a shield to those who walk in integrity, guarding the paths of justice and watching over the way of his saints. - Proverbs 2:6-8

Jesus said to him, "I am the way, and the truth, and the life. No one comes to the Father except through me."- John 14:6

# Day 33: Forgiveness

> *For if you forgive others their trespasses, your heavenly Father will also forgive you, but if you do not forgive others their trespasses, neither will your Father forgive your trespasses.*
>
> *Matthew 6:14-15*

You may have heard it said that "bitterness is like drinking poison and expecting someone else to die." Bitterness creates a wall around the heart that makes it harder to give and receive love. There was a time when I was so very bitter against a dear friend of mine. I sat in my pride, believing that she was the problem. I was so blinded to my own sin and my ability to hurt and tear down that the only thing I could see was my pain. For over a year, I refused to offer true forgiveness by nursing a grudge and viewing her through that lens. This bitterness robbed me of my joy and interrupted my peace. It stung and threatened our friendship because we could not communicate openly and honestly. When I finally confessed my sin to the Lord and allowed Him to break down the walls, it was as if a dam were loosened in my soul. I was able to breathe again and found rest.

Forgiveness is a critical part of fostering. Not only do we need to be able to forgive others when we feel they have wronged us, but we need to be able to ask for forgiveness when we have wronged others. It is easy to sit on our high horse and believe the lie that says that we are the heroes in this story. After all, we are the ones who have welcomed children from hard places into our homes, right? We are the ones making the sacrifices in ways that no one can see. We are the ones who are dealing with the effects of trauma from scars that occurred long before we entered the picture.

And yet we are only a small part of the grand story that God is weaving in the lives of our children and their biological families. We are not the Savior. There is only one Savior, and we cannot do what He has already done. We must walk in humility in order to have a right view of ourselves. When we do this, forgiveness becomes much easier as we remember that we are no better than anyone else.

In this journey, we will sin against someone else, and someone else will sin against us. We will for sure sin against our children, and they will for sure sin against us. The same can be said for our spouse, our well-meaning friends, biological parents, case workers—you get the picture. This whole journey is full of people who are flawed and will make mistakes.

But God offers us the gift of forgiveness, and this is a gift we can offer others. When we walk in forgiveness, we live freely and are able to commune with Him. Let us not allow bitterness to hold us back from walking in peace with others and with our Father.

**Prayer**

Father, forgive me for not forgiving others. Forgive me for thinking that I know better than You do. Forgive me for not allowing Your peace to reign in my heart and for holding on to the bitterness that chokes out life. Help me to see myself clearly and remember my need so that I can rest in Your forgiveness that You have so generously given to me. Help me to know that You are good and that Your love is mighty and strong enough to conquer everything. I so badly want vengeance and justice on my own terms, but Your word says that vengeance belongs to You. I want to believe that, Lord. Help me to forgive as You have forgiven me. And help me to ask for forgiveness when I have wronged others.

**Scripture to Declare**

Vengeance is mine, and recompense, for the time when their foot shall slip; for the day of their calamity is at hand, and their doom comes swiftly.' For the Lord will vindicate his people and have compassion on his servants, when he sees that their power is gone and there is none remaining, bond or free. -Deuteronomy 32:35-36

Repay no one evil for evil, but give thought to do what is honorable in the sight of all. - Romans 12:17

# Day 34: Humility

*Pride goes before destruction, and a haughty spirit before a fall. - Proverbs 16:18*

    As I shared before, my husband and I were way in over our heads with our first placement. We believed that things would just be more simple than they were. If you have kids from hard places in your home, you should be able to pour a lot of love on them and then they will be fine, right? And since their parents were struggling to care for them, we were at least doing a better job than they were, so things shouldn't be so difficult, right? I am sure you know that nothing could be further from the truth. We did not realize it then, but we had put ourselves in the place of Jesus by thinking that we could be their saviors.

Within the foster care journey, humility is of the utmost importance. It has been said that pride is the root of all sin, and this I know to be true. For when we sin, we say to God, "What You said isn't really true. What You said does not apply to me. I know better than You." It is so tempting to believe lies about our self-importance when we are foster parents, isn't it? We say that we want to fight for the whole family, and we so badly believe in the power of reunification and family preservation. But if we are being truly honest, we also struggle with thoughts like these:

"If my child's biological parents had done a better job, I wouldn't be dealing with _____."

"I would never do that/make that choice. How could they do that?"

"I am such a better parent than my child's biological parents. They're not even trying."

The beauty of foster care is that it reminds us of our need for the Gospel. The Gospel of Jesus Christ says that we have all sinned and fall short of the glory of God. There is nothing that we can do to earn a place in heaven. There is nothing we can do to make God love us any more or any less. The only way to salvation is through faith in the finished work of Jesus on the cross. There is no other means of eternal life.

When we remind ourselves of this truth, we no longer see the biological parents of our kids as our enemies. We see them as fellow image bearers who need reminding (or perhaps need to learn for the first time) that they were created to glorify God. We see our interactions with them as opportunities to show them the love of Christ and treat them with dignity and respect.

In the world of foster care, we have a very real lack of control. Our lives are dictated by the decisions of case workers, judges, and attorneys. We have been given the opportunity to advocate for our children for such a time as this by standing for the truth and walking alongside them through what will most likely be one of, if not the hardest, seasons in their lives. This calling is not to be taken lightly. When our pride enters into the situation, we do nothing but divide and alienate. But when we approach it with kindness and humility, we remember our need for the Savior, and rest in knowing that the ground is level at the foot of the cross.

## Prayer

Father, I know that You are above all things. You made all things, and we live and move and have our being in You. I do not want to see myself as the savior. Your Son is the Savior. I often think that if I just get more organized or if other people just "get it together," my life would be easier. But You have not called me to an easy life of comfort. You have called me to follow You and to take up my cross. I ask that You help me to do so with humility and peace. Help me be kind and to not think too highly of myself. I know that You have given me the opportunity to be a part of my children's lives and that You have entrusted me with their care. Help me to not take that for granted and to remember that You are my source of strength and help. Thank You for the way You love me and show me Your great grace each and every day.

## Scripture to Declare

Put on then, as God's chosen ones, holy and beloved, compassionate hearts, kindness, humility, meekness, and patience, bearing with one another and, if one has a complaint against another, forgiving each other; as the Lord has forgiven you, so you also must forgive. And above all these put on love, which binds everything together in perfect harmony. And let the peace of Christ rule in your hearts, to which indeed you were called in one body. And be thankful. - Colossians 3:12-15

# Day 35: Contentment

*The Lord will fulfill his purpose for me; your steadfast love, O Lord, endures forever. Do not forsake the work of your hands. - Psalm 138:8*

    I am convinced that one of the greatest tools of the enemy is an ungrateful heart. And on the flip side, a great tool in the life of a believer is to sit before God with gratitude and praise, no matter the circumstances. It is tempting for me to believe many lies as a foster parent. Because my motherhood journey looks different than my peers' journeys, it is easy to compare and feel lonely because our family is so unique. So many thoughts can flood my mind and steal my joy:

*My friends don't understand what it means to parent a child from trauma.*

*How in the world am I supposed to manage so many needs within my home?*

*Why did the case manager ignore my call* again?! *I need her help!*

When I allow thoughts like these to settle in my mind and spirit, I sow seeds of discontentment. I become hyper-focused on that which I think I lack. Everything becomes all about me and my issues. But when I choose contentment, my heart is instantly lighter. My mind is free of the clutter and chaos, and I can rest in God's perfect peace.

The journey of foster care is difficult and complicated. There are many layers and aspects of this journey that are so unfamiliar to many. It can feel heavy and burdensome. But when we lay those burdens at the feet of Jesus, we find that His yoke is easy and His burden is light. Many of us approach the journey of foster care with prayer and maybe even fasting. However, when we find ourselves in the thick of taxing situations, we are crying out for an escape. The assignment given to us by God seems too difficult to bear, and we want out. We want to get back to life as we knew it and not be part of such heavy work. But God has greater plans for us. He makes a way for us to know Him in the midst of the circumstances we are in, and that is through contentment. We can know Him through our attitude of gratitude.

1 Thessalonians 5:18 says, "Give thanks in all circumstances; for this is the will of God in Christ Jesus for you." God desires for us to be grateful and to live with the knowledge that He is working, even when we do not feel like He is. When you are tempted to complain and grumble about your day, remember that there were days when you prayed for the life that you have now. There were times when you couldn't even imagine the privilege of leading the life you live. There were days when your home was not filled with the constant chattering and the door slamming and the crying. But there were also days when your home was not filled with the belly laughs and the joy and the beautiful sanctification that occurs when one lays down their life for another.

To be content is to recognize that God's ways are greater and that He is good. To be content is to understand and know that God is sovereign and that every good and perfect gift comes from Him. He is kind and generous and loves to bless us. Our definition of blessing is often tied to material gains, but the blessing we receive from Him is when we are made more like Him. We are made more like Him when we sacrifice for others who have nothing to give us in return. Is this not the picture of foster care? When we consider the great gift we have received as foster parents, we can only give thanks for all that God is doing in and through us to advance His kingdom and make His name great.

**Prayer**

Father, I admit that sometimes it is hard for me to be content. It is hard for me to know how to give thanks when I feel defeated, overwhelmed, and tired. But I know that when I least feel like it are the moments that I need to come to You and admit my need once again. Help me not to be embarrassed or ashamed of my need for You. I want to love You above all else, and I know that a heart of gratitude will help me to do that. Your ways are higher than mine and Your thoughts are greater. You have given me everything I need to live a life of godliness through your Holy Spirit. A grateful heart is part of that, and I want to give You thanks—no matter what. Help me to be content with all that You are and all You have given me, even when things do not look the way I thought they would.

**Scripture to Declare**

But godliness with contentment is great gain, for we brought nothing into the world, and we cannot take anything out of the world. But if we have food and clothing, with these we will be content. - 1 Timothy 6:6-8

And whatever you do, in word or deed, do everything in the name of the Lord Jesus, giving thanks to God the Father through him. - Colossians 3:17

There is therefore now no condemnation for those who are in Christ Jesus. - Romans 8:1

# Day 36: Guilt and Shame

*There is therefore now no condemnation for those who are in Christ Jesus. - Romans 8:1*

Why would anyone want to feel like this? It's awful! No wonder no one wants to be a foster parent!" A friend of mine said these words while we were at a small group gathering of foster and adoptive parents after a hard season, and I completely understood and was able to empathize with her. Because as a foster parent, guilt and shame are two feelings that unfortunately try to creep in and steal the joy of being made more like Christ through the sanctification of loving children from hard places. The range of emotions that are felt as a foster parent run the gamut from joy and wonder to devastating guilt and shame.

Guilt is felt when you have committed a certain action that has negative consequences (sin) while shame is felt when you are humiliated and upset by that behavior. Guilt is healthy—it enables you to turn around and repent. Shame can cause a vicious cycle in which you feel a sense of distress about who you are as a person. Guilt is always tied to a specific action that needs correcting, while shame is often tied to your sense of identity.

For example, let's say that I lose it with my children because they won't stop talking and are constantly asking me questions. (This is completely hypothetical of course, because I am the picture of patience.) When I lose it and snap, I immediately feel a sense of guilt—I shouldn't have reacted in such a harsh way. They are just kids. They need attention and love and care, and I can give it to them with patience and kindness, even when it is exhausting. I can apologize and ask for their forgiveness, and we can begin again. But shame takes this a step further and says that I am a bad mom for losing it. I can never do anything right. I am always too harsh, and I am messing them up due to my lack of self-control and patience. They will never understand God's love for them because I cannot show it to them with perfect consistency.

Do you see the spiral that occurs when we allow ourselves to enter into shame? 2 Corinthians 7:10 says, "For godly grief produces a repentance that leads to salvation without regret, whereas worldly grief produces death." When we are convicted by the Holy Spirit about our actions, we can move forward in a healthy way toward a new way of living. But when we are sorrowful in a way that is focused on ourselves and that turns inward in a self-absorbed way, we help no one.

Our children often have come from places that may have confused guilt and shame as well. They may not understand how to take personal responsibility for things because they have been afraid of getting in trouble. And rightfully so, as discipline may have held extreme consequences and harsh punishments instead of natural consequences and gentle leading to the truth. It is so important that we learn how to differentiate between guilt and shame and walk in the freedom of the Holy Spirit so that we can lead our children to do the same.

If we speak in the language of shame—"You should know better" or "Why do I have to tell you this over and over?" we are not making space for our children to grow. We cannot allow our expectations of their behaviors to influence how we parent. Instead, we must submit our desires for them to the Lord and ask Him to help us love and lead them well. When we know whose we are, we will be able to move past our own guilt and shame and give them a perspective that is rooted in the truth of His word.

**Prayer**

Father, I know the language of shame well. It is filled with unmet expectations, frustrations, and offenses. I do not want to speak this language to myself or to my children. I want to speak the language of love, kindness, and mercy. Your word says that You discipline those whom You love, so I know that it is a healthy thing to experience guilt and sorrow when I sin against You. You take sin seriously, and You sent Your Son to die for my sins. Help me not to take Your sacrifice on the cross for granted. You are more than enough for me, and I know that You have good things in store for me when I come to You in repentance. Help me to model this for my children by asking for their forgiveness when I sin against them. Help them to know the importance of taking responsibility for their actions while also embracing your infinite grace and mercy.

**Scripture to Declare**

In you, O Lord, do I take refuge; let me never be put to shame!- Psalm 71:1

If I must boast, I will boast of the things that show my

weakness.- 2 Corinthians   11:30

# Day 37: Boundaries

*Lord, you alone are my portion and my cup; you make my lot secure. The boundary lines have fallen for me in pleasant places; surely I have a delightful inheritance. - Psalm 16:5-6*

When my husband and I were first married, we read the book *Boundaries* by authors Henry Cloud and John Townsend. It was incredibly eye-opening for us. If you haven't read it, I highly recommend it. Here is the gist of the book—we all need to understand the importance of creating boundaries within our relationships—not just our most important ones, but in every relationship in our lives. Boundaries are a set of guidelines put in place for how you will interact with people. For instance, in our marriage, we do not yell and scream at one another when we are upset. That is a boundary line that we do not cross. In our family, we have boundaries for the things we will and will not watch on television. We have boundaries with our employers as to how often we allow work to take us away from family. Boundaries help us to know what to say yes to and what to say no to. Every yes means that you are saying no to something else. This is not a bad thing! We cannot be all things to all people.

As foster parents, we tend to think that we can do it all. But the truth is, we are limited. And that is a good thing. We absolutely cannot do everything on our own, yet we try. We want to be able to solve all the problems and save all the children. But we can't. Having boundaries ensures us that we are reminded of our limitations and able to give glory to God for the ways that He empowers us to do the work of foster care. We need Him every day in order to help us know how to love and care for children from hard places.

When we were in the process of obtaining our foster care license, we completed copious amounts of paperwork. There was one particular page that was so difficult—you know the one. This page lists all of the possible behavior and health issues one could think of that a child might have when they walk through your doors. It was hard for my husband and I to check yes or no for each of the issues. But in doing so, we were being honest about what we could and could not handle in that stage of our lives. The boundaries have changed over the past couple years, as we are in a different season. As we have added children to our family, we have taken steps to reevaluate what we feel we are equipped to do. Of course, God always has a sense of humor. We all know that we rarely get all of the information we need to know about a child in order to make an informed decision as to whether (we think) they would be a good fit in our family. But the Holy Spirit instructs us and helps us to know what to do when we do not have all the information we would like to have.

The beautiful thing about boundaries is that they are not hard and fast rules. God helps us to know how to navigate these often complicated and weighty decisions. He knows the desires of our hearts, along with our doubts and fears. He also knows that we are capable of so much more than we think we are when we walk in step with the Holy Spirit. So fellow foster parent, know that God has a perfect plan in store for you that may or may not include what you had in mind. We can find comfort in knowing that His ways are better and higher, and He will never leave or forsake us.

**Prayer**

Father, I know that it is important to have boundaries. I know that in order to care for our family well, we must trust that You have a perfect plan in store. Thank You for the limitations placed on us as human beings. Thank You that we cannot save any children, and that is not what You have called us to do. Thank You for the way You work and for Your divine wisdom that helps us know how to make decisions. Please help us to listen to Your voice so that we can look to You in all things, knowing that You will guide and direct us as we surrender to You.

**Scripture to Declare**

For consider your calling, brothers: not many of you were wise according to worldly standards, not many were powerful, not many were of noble birth. But God chose what is foolish in the world to shame the wise; God chose what is weak in the world to shame the strong; God chose what is low and despised in the world, even things that are not, to bring to nothing things that are, so that no human being might boast in the presence of God. And because of him you are in Christ Jesus, who became to us wisdom from God, righteousness and sanctification and redemption, so that, as it is written, "Let the one who boasts, boast in the Lord."- 1 Corinthians 1:26-31

# Day 38: Grace of God

*But I do not account my life of any value nor as precious to myself, if only I may finish my course and the ministry that I received from the Lord Jesus, to testify to the gospel of the grace of God. - Acts 20:24*

Grace is unmerited favor, a gift given that is completely undeserved. When we take a look at our lives as foster parents, the grace of God abounds. Just this weekend, my husband and I went away for our anniversary. I was battling so many emotions in the last few hours—sadness that our little getaway was almost over and excitement to be back and see my kids. You know how it is! When we walked through the door, our kids had prepared the sweetest surprise for our anniversary. It literally took my breath away, and I couldn't stop crying. It was overwhelming—I just kept saying to my husband, "Aren't you glad that we didn't give up? We could have missed this. People just don't know how rich foster care can be." He jokingly said back to me, "Maybe we shouldn't share this with other foster parents. They might get jealous! On second thought, maybe we should tell others so that they become foster parents, too!"

The beauty of God's grace is that it seems too good to be true, but it is true. It is the reality of our lives, and at moments, it can be breathtakingly beautiful. But the most stunning part of grace is that it is not earned, it is given. We cannot perform our way to grace. God gives grace upon grace, and we are but the recipients of this tenderness. I've heard it said that until we understand what we are capable of, we will not truly appreciate God's grace. When we are tempted to lose it with the kid who is having a hard time, we must remember His grace. When we are comparing our parenting journey with our friends, we must remember His grace.

Paul writes in 2 Corinthians 12:9: "But he said to me, 'My grace is sufficient for you, for my power is made perfect in weakness.' Therefore, I will boast all the more gladly of my weaknesses, so that the power of Christ may rest upon me." Boasting in our weakness looks like admitting when we need help. It means that we ask for prayer instead of trying to stuff down the emotions that keep coming for us. It means taking time to do the things we love and caring for our bodies properly in order to continue to serve and love well.

The gift of God's grace is evident in our lives as foster parents as He allows us the great privilege of learning from and coming alongside children in care. As a foster parent, people often say to me, "Wow, those kids are so blessed to be in your home." But we know the truth of this statement—kids are never blessed to be in care. The fact that a child is in care means that a grave tragedy has occurred and that his or her life has been turned upside down. Yes, we can say thank You for the grace and providence of God to give this child a loving home for a season. But the real blessing lies in the lessons children will teach us with their lives. What most people do not know about fostering is that the greatest recipients are not the children, but rather the foster parents. I cannot even begin to say what the journey of fostering has done in my relationship with the Lord. To see Him as the Heavenly Father and understand His heart for the vulnerable — it changes everything.

**Prayer**

Father, thank You for Your abundant grace. Thank You that when I am weak and afraid, You call me by name. You say that I can trust You with everything, and I know this is true because You have made Your faithfulness known to me time and time again. Help me to rest in Your grace, knowing that You will give it if I just come to You and ask. Help me to embrace my weakness and know that You are with me. Help me to recognize Your glimpses of grace in the midst of the mundane, the scary, and the tumultuous, for You alone are good.

**Scripture to Declare**

Let us then with confidence draw near to the throne of grace, that we may receive mercy and find grace to help in time of need. - Hebrews 4:16

The Lord bless you and keep you; the Lord make his face to shine upon you and be gracious to you; the Lord lift up his countenance upon you and give you peace. - Numbers 6:24-26

# Day 39: His Sovereignty

*Great is our Lord, and abundant in power; his understanding is beyond measure.* - Psalm 147:5

There is nothing like the foster care journey, is there? One moment, you're laughing like crazy as you run around in your yard with kids who you just met. Fast forward a couple months, and you're crying on the floor of your closet as you realize that they are leaving your home and you cannot do a thing about it. The beauty and the brokenness of foster care chase you down and won't let you go, inviting you to sit in the middle of the tension of unmet longings and expectations. As foster parents, we are faced with the task of loving and caring for the vulnerable—children and adults alike. It is exceptionally difficult and extremely beautiful.

Most of us would admit that the trials we have faced as foster parents are ones that we would have run away from had we known they were coming. And yet most of us would also admit that they were worth it. No, we wouldn't want to do it all over again. But we can look back and see that God's mighty hand made a difference not only in the lives of the children we serve, but in ours as well. We can see that His faithfulness, goodness, and love were woven throughout stories that we have the privilege of entering into.

The journey of foster care is not a path of least resistance, and it is not a path for the faint of heart. It is one paved with blood, sweat, and tears—quite literally. When we reflect on our calling and what God has done in our lives as a result, we can only give thanks to Him for the ways in which He chooses to work through our surrendered hearts. God sent His Son to earth to come into the middle of the mess and make old things new. He came that we might have life in the midst of circumstances that appear to be dead. He came that we might know His goodness in the midst of unthinkable tragedy and betrayal. He came to restore us and make us completely new.

His ways are not our ways. His thoughts are not our thoughts. Each person in the midst of the foster care journey is an image bearer of God. He created each one to bear witness to His name and give glory to Him alone. The glory of the cross invites us to remember God's goodness to us and His divine intention in choosing us to be a part of His family. Each one of us who is in Christ has been adopted into His eternal family and now bears witness to the good work He has done.

The work of foster care, at its core, is reflective of the gospel. Jesus said that He came to seek and save the lost. At some point, we were the ones who were lost. But the love of another person who spoke the truth to us brought us from darkness to light. We have the privilege of doing just that when we speak hope and healing into the lives of the children, families, and various professionals that comprise the foster care community. We have the joy of watching God work miracles before our very eyes, often when we thought that all hope was lost.

This is foster care. This is the gospel of Jesus Christ — to leave the ninety-nine to find the one and give our all that more may know Him and walk with Him in life and peace for eternity.

**Prayer**

Father, thank You for allowing me to be a part of Your great work on earth through foster care. Thank You for impressing this work upon my heart and for making me aware of this crisis within our country. Thank You for giving me the ability to care for children. I ask that You help me not to take this responsibility for granted and that You enable me to not just view it as a "good deed," but rather as a privilege and honor as a follower of Christ. I pray that You allow the children who enter my home to enter into Your family. This is my highest hope and the joy of my heart—to watch as children walk from darkness into the light as they encounter the love of their Heavenly Father. Please also give me opportunities to share the truth of the Gospel with others who we encounter on this journey - case managers, CASA volunteers, birth parents, and anyone else whom You place on our path. Thank You for the joy that is found in doing Your will. Thank You for Your abundant life and for the way You give grace upon grace for the work You have called me to. Everything I am is Yours.

**Scripture to Declare**

When the Lord restored the fortunes of Zion, we were like those who dream. Then our mouth was filled with laughter, and our tongue with shouts of joy; then they said among the nations, "The Lord has done great things for them." The Lord has done great things for us; we are glad. Restore our fortunes, O Lord, like streams in the Negeb! Those who sow in tears shall reap with shouts of joy! He who goes out weeping, bearing the seed for sowing, shall come home with shouts of joy, bringing his sheaves with him. - Psalm 126:1-6

# Day 40: Facts vs. Truth

*I have no greater joy than to hear that my children are walking in the truth.* -
3 John 1:4

    One of the greatest gifts my husband has given me through our marriage is the understanding that facts matter. When we were first married, I believed that it was perfectly normal and acceptable to allow my feelings to dictate a lot of my decisions and thought processes. As you can imagine, this was a very volatile way to live. Of course, there is nothing wrong with having emotions. God Himself gave them to us. In His word, He models how to feel our emotions in a healthy way. He expresses anger at true injustice. He mourns with those who mourn. He rejoices with those who rejoice.

    As stated several times throughout this book, the foster care journey is full of emotions. These emotions often wage war within us (and our children), fighting to express themselves and come out from hiding. There are myriad opportunities for us to succumb to feelings of hopelessness and despair. When the birth parents are not cooperating with the case plan. When the case worker is not understanding or kind during moments of crisis. When the children are struggling for survival. When life outside of foster care turns upside down and you just don't know if you can take one more thing falling apart.

A practice that has helped me in this journey is filtering the facts and my feelings through the truth of God's word. The facts of life can be harsh and difficult to process. For instance, the facts of our children's lives can seem hopeless. I may look at a child's life and say, "The fact is that he is extremely behind in school, and there are so many things he doesn't know that he needs to know." In response to this fact, my feelings may say, "I feel helpless and don't know how to make this situation better. He will never catch up."

But when filtered through the lens of truth, I can say with confidence, "Nothing is impossible with God. He is able to do exceedingly and abundantly more than all that we can think or imagine, and I believe that He can do this in my child's life. I choose to trust Him." Within a matter of seconds, the facts and feelings no longer seem so overwhelming. This is the power of the Word of God that is living and active.

Let us cling to the truth, knowing that our God is capable, powerful, and willing to heal, save, and restore.

**Prayer**

Father, sometimes the facts of the circumstances in my life seem overwhelming. They can point to despair and disappointment instead of hope and healing. I do not want to be cynical or believe that You are not capable of making all things new. Your word says that You can make a way in the wilderness. Your Son died on the cross in order to bring life where death has reigned. I choose to trust You, no matter what the circumstances say. I choose to rest in Your truth and know that no matter what, You are good. Help me to believe and rest in You when it seems like there is no hope. I want to trust You to do what only You can do, which is redeem all that has been lost. I thank You in advance for the work You are going to do in my heart and in the hearts of all who are a part of our foster care journey. To You be the glory forever.

**Scripture to Declare**

The threshing floors shall be full of grain; the vats shall overflow with wine and oil. I will restore to you the years that the swarming locust has eaten, the hopper, the destroyer, and the cutter, my great army, which I sent among you. You shall eat in plenty and be satisfied, and praise the name of the Lord your God, who has dealt wondrously with you. And my people shall never again be put to shame. You shall know that I am in the midst of Israel, and that I am the Lord your God and there is none else. And my people shall never again be put to shame. - Joel 2:24-27

# Conclusion

I've heard it said that when you decide to write a book on any given topic, you walk through seasons that allow you to live out your message. That has definitely been the case for my other books, and this book is no exception. This message is one I believe in so strongly because I have seen the wonders of answered prayer in the lives of our family time and time again. While writing this book, our family's structure shifted as we added another child to our mix via foster care. And with that addition, our whole lives shifted. I have told so many people that with the addition of this third child, my brain just quit. Of course that is a little exaggerative, but wow am I tired! If you're reading this book, I know you can relate.

While I started this book in 2019, the majority of its content has been written in 2020. The year 2020 has been one for the history books, as we all know. There has been loss, heartache, confusion, destruction, and devastation on so many levels. No one has been left untouched by the trials that have plagued our world. It has been so very easy to look at the world around us and think, "How much more, Lord? We cannot take one more hard thing."

And yet within the brokenness He has offered so much peace. He has given us reminders that He is with us and that He will never leave or forsake us. He has shown us that even in the midst of great suffering, He never changes. And isn't this what we need most of all? To know that He is God, regardless of our circumstances? To believe that He is good, no matter the breaking news that threatens our hope?

As foster parents, we have the great privilege of walking alongside children and families who need the hope of Christ to break through their lives. And the fact is, we need the hope of Christ, too. We each have brokenness that we carry, and pain is pain, no matter how big or small.

We know that what once was broken can be put back together and made beautiful. He gives us eyes to see and ears to hear if only we surrender to Him. Our circumstances may threaten to rob us of our joy and confidence, but the Lord who is mighty can restore and redeem anything. As we walk through such uncertainty that plagues our current world climate, we can rest in the peace of a God who has carried us before and will continue to carry us, no matter what comes our way.

# Acknowledgments

    I absolutely love writing. It is such a gift in times of confusion and stress to be able to write down my thoughts and feelings, often in raw form. Somehow, when those thoughts come together as a book, the Lord uses it to encourage others. This privilege and responsibility is not lost on me. I hope and pray that the words in this book have encouraged you to keep going.

    Thank you to my incredible husband for walking this journey out in every season with such steadfastness and patience. I can't imagine living life any other way than with you by my side. Thank you so much to my foster mama friends who encouraged me to write this book and share it with others. You are all incredible women whom I am blessed to know! Thank you to our friends, family, and care team who support us in so many ways so that we can continue to foster. The meals, babysitting, and prayer support you provide are priceless gifts to us.

    Thank you to Anna Crouse for the incredibly beautiful cover design. You literally took what was in my brain and put it on paper.

You are so gifted!

All praise to the Lord for His amazing grace and kindness in allowing me the honor of mothering children through biology and foster care. What a precious gift. May I steward it well.

If you enjoyed this book, would you share it with a friend? You can also find me on Instagram at @jessicanmathisen and use the hashtag #fosteringprayerbook to connect with others who have read the book!

Made in United States
Orlando, FL
04 March 2023